T0322230

ROSEN'S ALMANAC

Weird and wonderful words *for every day of the year*

MICHAEL ROSEN

EBURY
PRESS

Ebury Press, an imprint of Ebury Publishing
One Embassy Gardens, 8 Viaduct Gdns,
Nine Elms, London SW11 7BW

Ebury Press is part of the Penguin Random House group of companies whose
addresses can be found at global.penguinrandomhouse.com

Penguin
Random House
UK

Copyright © Michael Rosen 2024
Illustrations © Andrzej Krauze 2024

'Another Christmas Poem' by Wendy Cope © Wendy Cope
and reproduced with the kind permission of Faber & Faber

Michael Rosen has asserted his right to be identified as the author of this Work
in accordance with the Copyright, Designs and Patents Act 1988

Every effort has been made to trace and contact copyright holders,
but if there are any inadvertent omissions, please contact us in order
to rectify any mistakes that are brought to our attention.

No part of this book may be used or reproduced in any manner for the purpose
of training artificial intelligence technologies or systems. In accordance with
Article 4(3) of the DSM Directive 2019/790, Penguin Random House
expressly reserves this work from the text and data mining exception.

First published by Ebury Press in 2024

www.penguin.co.uk

A CIP catalogue record for this book is available from the British Library

ISBN 9781529148916

Printed and bound in Great Britain by Clays Ltd, Elcograf S.p.A.

The authorised representative in the EEA is Penguin Random House Ireland,
Morrison Chambers, 32 Nassau Street, Dublin D02 YH68.

Penguin Random House is committed to a sustainable future for our business,
our readers and our planet. This book is made from
Forest Stewardship Council® certified paper.

MIX
Paper | Supporting
responsible forestry
FSC
www.fsc.org   FSC® C018179

For Emma

INTRODUCTION

Welcome.

Are we who we are because of what other people say to us and what we ourselves say? It seems like it, though we would have to factor in what others 'do' to us and what we do too.

We looked at this on BBC Radio 4's *Word of Mouth*, the programme I present. I put out a request on social media as follows:

> Coming up on *Word of Mouth*: inherited words and phrases.
>
> We want to hear the word or phrase you've inherited from someone, family or friend, for a special edition featuring your stories! Tell us the bit of language you've picked up and who, where and when it came from!

We had over 1,600 replies.

On the programme itself, I talked to Rob Drummond, Professor of Sociolinguistics at Manchester Metropolitan University and author of *You're All Talk: Why We Are What We Speak*.

Our conversation set me thinking about how we understand language. It's fairly easy to pull bits of language away from people and look at these bits as if they are things we can put under a microscope. We can even talk of language as if it's a thing that can do things to us. I might hear myself say, echoing my days at school, 'English keeps the verb next to the subject of the sentence' (meaning that we say or write things like 'I wandered lonely as a cloud' where 'I' is the 'subject' and 'wandered' is the verb). But actually it's not 'English' doing that, it's us! We are the speakers and writers.

What follows, then, is a collection of examples of living language – the poetry of the people, if you like. The spine of the book consists of the words and phrases that people (including me) remember from home and friends. I use a clumsy phrase to describe this: 'language-in-use' to distinguish it from neat, cold language on its own.

We use these home words and phrases as part of our lives, in nearly all our activities and even in a lot of our thought. Yes, we are what we eat, but we are also what we speak, hear, write and read. And yet in saying that, I'm surely missing out a dimension: all that language, all those uses, have histories. There are the immediate histories of who told us these words and expressions. Then, like our family trees, those words and expressions go back through our families and the societies our ancestors lived in for hundreds and thousands of years.

Thanks to the great *Oxford English Dictionary*, a dictionary based on quotations of words in context, we can and should keep in focus the fact that those ancestral words and expressions were said and heard, written and read by real people in real situations. No matter how many books are written *about* language, we should always remember that language is *ours*. We make it for our purposes.

That's why this book wanders about all over the place, full of hundreds of examples, quirks and surprises. In that, I hope it'll remind you that how we use language is not a simple, regular process any more than identity, behaviour or culture are simple, regular processes.

As the book is an almanac, you can use it like a calendar if you want. Now that many of us have become expert at surfing, you can be non-chronological and surf it too. This way of reading and particularly the sheer amount of it has expanded one way in which we get knowledge: we create our own networks and pathways between the topics we surf. Perhaps this is changing how we think?

I can hear in my head people using the word 'browsing' as if it's trivial or, at best, the starters that come before the main meal of solid reading. If you dip in here (as I do with my hummus), rest assured I won't be looking over your shoulder making demands that you read in any other way. Quite the contrary. How about another axiom? We are the links we make.

And one final note. You will come across some Yiddish words and expressions in the book. They are spelled that way because there is a standardised way of spelling Yiddish when using Roman letters. This is called 'transliteration' because Yiddish is traditionally written using Hebrew letters. You can find the standardised transliterations in YIVO's *Modern English-Yiddish Yiddish-English Dictionary*, first published in 1968. YIVO is an acronym based on 'yidisher visnshaftlekher institut', which was founded in 1925 in Poland before the Holocaust forced its relocation to New York in 1940. There are many non-standardised ways of writing Yiddish that people make up, improvise or have learned from someone else. I have no problem with these but as I'm learning Yiddish, I'm doing my best to conform to what I'm being taught. It's a little bit like the variety of spellings that we find in Shakespeare's time – full of improvisation and invention.

Almanac

What is an almanac? And where does the word come from?

One of the first people to use the word 'almanac' in writing was Geoffrey Chaucer. He wrote several books other than *The Canterbury Tales*, one of them being *A Treatise on the Astrolabe*, which was completed in 1391. Mostly people haven't found the *Treatise* as much fun as *The Canterbury Tales* as it doesn't have stories of talking chickens or people having sex up a tree. However, in the *Treatise*, Chaucer writes: 'A table of the verray Moeuyng of the Mone from howre to howre, euery day & in euery signe, after thin Almenak.' In modern spelling, this translates to: 'A table of the very moving of the moon, from hour to hour, every day and in every sign, after thine Almanac' ('after thine' meaning 'according to your').

If you think that the word 'almanac' doesn't sound or look like a word of Germanic or Latin origin, you'd be right, just as you would for hundreds of other words in English – for example, pyjamas, robot, shampoo, thug, caravan, hammock, ketchup and tattoo.

The *Oxford English Dictionary* (*OED*) suggests that the word was first used in English from Old French and/or what the *OED* calls 'post-classical Latin' (the Latin spoken or written after Roman times). And, burrowing still deeper, those Old French or Latin speakers and writers took 'almanac' from people speaking and writing 'Spanish Arabic'. 'Al' meant 'the' and 'manāk' meant 'calendar'. These pathways speak of merchants and scholars moving about medieval Europe, exchanging goods and ideas. Chaucer himself was a great borrower – *The Canterbury Tales* hums with the stories, scenes, ideas, language and literary forms from worlds way beyond England. Language and culture are hardly ever monocultural.

Clearly, you don't have in your hands something that is only or simply a calendar. People started calling this kind of book an almanac too, in the first part of the nineteenth century, and by the early twentieth you could buy *The Motorists' Almanac for 1917 Anno Domini: Containing Much Entertainment and Not a Few Facts of Concern and Interest to All Intelligent Motorists.*

So what follows is indeed an almanac and I hope you'll find that it's 'containing much entertainment and not a few facts of concern and interest to all' … whoever you are.

Days of the Week

But before we dive in, let's consider for a moment the origins of our names for the days of the week. In Roman times, the days were named after the classical planets of ancient Greek astrology, in this order:

Sun (Helios) – Sunday
Moon (Selene) – Monday
Mars (Ares) – Tuesday
Mercury (Hermes) – Wednesday'
Jupiter (Zeus) – Thursday
Venus (Aphrodite) – Friday
Saturn (Cronus) – Saturday

This has worked out for us like this:

- Sunday is sun day and is an English translation of the Latin phrase *diēs Sōlis* – day of the sun.

- Monday is moon day and is equivalent to the Latin name *diēs Lūnae* – day of the moon.

- Tuesday is Tiw's day or Tyr's day. The Old English god Tiw or the Norse god Tyr was a one-handed god associated with war. The name of the day is related to the Latin name *diēs Mārtis* – day of Mars (the Roman god of war).

- Wednesday is Woden's day. Woden was the chief god in the pagan Germanic pantheon.

- Thursday is Thor's day. Thor was the god of thunder and this relates to Latin *diēs Iovis* – day of Jupiter (the Roman god of thunder – amongst other things).

- Friday is the day of the pagan Germanic goddess Frigg. It relates to Latin *diēs Veneris* – day of Venus (goddess of love, beauty, sex and fertility).

- Saturday is named after the Roman god Saturn. In Latin, it was *diēs Sāturnī* – day of Saturn.

January

It can seem strange that some of our most familiar words hold within them threads that pull us back hundreds and thousands of years. That's an obvious thing to observe when we use, say, a Latin phrase like 'ad nauseam' – but hiding in the word 'January' is a link to a Roman god. As we shall see, we surround ourselves with ancient deities in our months, festivals and days of the week. A Martian might think we were secret pagans.

Janus is the god behind January. Statues of this Roman god show him to be two-faced – not in the sense of being duplic-itous and deceitful, but in the sense of being both beginning and ending. He was the god who oversaw the ends of wars and conflicts: the god of war and peace then.

Traditionally, in ancient Rome, his image was mounted on gates or on walls so that he could look both outwards and inwards, forwards and backwards. So he's a perfect god for the New Year, as he can look back at the old year and forwards to the new one.

The name Janus comes from a word meaning 'door' – which we preserve to this day in the word 'janitor' and the Scots version 'janny'.

The Romans called January 'Ianuarius' and the people who spoke Old English (inaccurately called the 'Anglo-Saxons'), would write 'ianuarius' next to the Old English word 'æfterra geola'. If that looks unlike anything you've ever seen before, it is in fact 'after yule' (the 'g' at the beginning of 'geola' is pronounced as a 'y').

In case you're wondering how the Latin 'I' at the beginning of 'Ianuarius' became a 'j' then think of 1066. The Norman French arrived at Hastings saying 'Janver' (with a hard 'j' sound as in 'jug'). This also explains why we say 'justice' not 'iustice' and 'judge' not 'iudge'.

To kick off this trip round our family sayings, let me rudely begin with some of my own. Have you noticed that when you dwell on the things your parents, grandparents and perhaps great-grandparents said, you are taken straight back to the sounds, smells and textures of the people, the rooms and the places where these things were spoken? Famously, Marcel Proust talked of how a little madeleine cake could feel as if it transported him back so we now talk of 'madeleine moments'. We could call these family sayings 'madeleine sayings'.

Here are some sayings that the Rosen family always comes back to:

– 'It's clearing from the east.' From camping holidays spent waiting for the rain to stop. This became the thing to say when quite clearly it was the opposite – pouring with rain, cloud cover everywhere.

– 'Have a bagel. Save the hole for me.'
My zeyde's (grandfather's) gag.

– 'Never believe a rumour till it's officially denied.'
One of my father's political sayings.

– 'The bigger the car, the bigger the bugger.'
One of my father's motorist's sayings.

'A few sayings of my dad's, who was from Staffordshire:

— "He called him everything bar a Christian" (describing someone's angry response to another's careless/reckless action).

— "They'd have given you that at the Bricklayer's" (any near
miss – his equivalent of "close but no cigar", referring to
his old local).

— "If I was in bed I wouldn't get up for no dinner" (whenever he was feeling particularly comfy).

— "The doctor says I can get up a bit tomorrow" (whenever
anyone asked how he was).

— "One volunteer is worth a dozen pressed men" (when he
was looking for me to give him a hand with something).'

Ian Allen

My brother once tried to buy some hankies in July and the
person serving said, 'We've got no call for hankies in summer.'
After that, he used it for whenever you couldn't get something
from a shop – or from anywhere else.

A saying that reminds me I was often in trouble:
The deputy head, Harrow Weald County Grammar,
1958 or so (she was born in the 1890s), said in a deeply

shocked, almost whispered voice: 'Great Scott, boy! You're for the high jump!'

It has been imported into family sayings ever since.

My father had a sliding scale of bother from a little to a lot for when he was complaining about the work he hadn't done:

- 'Oy am I in tsirres!' (a little bit of bother)

- 'Oy am I in shtuck!' (quite a lot of bother)

- 'Oy am I in dr'erd!' (in really a lot of bother)

But the worst and without the 'oy': 'I'm in mittendrinen!' (total bother).

It's been a useful guideline my whole life.

Many things in my father's life seemed to revolve around his 'kishkes' (Yiddish for guts). 'I'm not going to bust my kishkes doing that'; 'since that meal, I've had nothing but trouble with my kishkes'; 'my kishkes are killing me'; and for a big emotional event – 'I felt it in my kishkes.'

When we meet each other, the first thing we do is say greeting words like 'Hi', 'How you doing?', 'Alright?' Some of them, like 'Alright?' are fine examples of how language is more than communication. We can't understand what we do with language if we think that every word we use has a neat boxed-up meaning which we transfer across to someone else who then opens the box. When I meet people on the street, we often say to each other, 'Alright?' but we're not usually communicating a concern or an interest as to whether the other person is actually alright. It's more of an affirmation that we know that we're friendly acquaintances. In this way, 'Alright?' doesn't mean 'Are you alright?' That's not what we're communicating.

Our unique family greetings make for fascinating reading. Here's one of my own:

My bubbe (Yiddish for granny) would say when we visited, 'Tatele, come to Bubbe!' (tatele literally means 'little dad'). When I say that, I can see the door to the flat, the look and smell of her purple cardigan, her long and loose silver hair (not like my friends' grannies' hair), and the perpetual look of seeming sadness, as if the world had been put together the wrong way round.

'My mother had some imaginary "ice breakers":

–   Which end of the bath do you sit?

–   We've got a breadmaking machine at home.

–   I hear they've had snow in Northampton.'

@richmondie

'My grandad used to say to us kids when we visited: "Come here, you pickled cabbage-faced article", which basically meant: come and give me a hug. No idea where it came from!'

@DebMacc

I'm studying Yiddish and we begin every class with 'Sholem aleykhem', to which the proper reply is 'Aleykem sholem'. That's followed by 'Vos makhstu', which means literally 'what are you doing?' but – like someone saying to you as you pass them by, 'Alright?' – you don't answer by saying what you're doing! The answer to 'Vos makhstu' is to say how you're feeling – OK, or a bit tired.

I've heard teenagers playing with phrases in similar ways: 'Sup!' (i.e. 'what's up?') of course doesn't have to be answered with an explanation of what is actually up.

Many young people in London are said to speak 'MLE' (multicultural London English) and for a while an older Caribbean phrase did the rounds: 'Waa gwaan?' (literally 'what's going on?'). TikTok informs me that there are plenty more: 'Waddup fam?', 'Yu good, innit?'

On English writing

Letters don't make sounds. We make sounds; letters are rough attempts to represent sounds-in-words. Why have I not just written 'sounds'? That's because the signs (letters and combinations of letters) are often word-specific. An example of this was George Bernard Shaw's gag (but it's a misplaced gag) that 'ghoti' could spell 'fish'. Try it, you could take 'gh' from the end of 'enough', the 'o' from 'women' and 'ti' from 'station'. Ah, but … 'gh' at the beginning of a word can never be equivalent to 'f', that's why I lifted it from the end of the word 'enough'. And the 'ti' at the end of 'ghoti' will never be pronounced as an equivalent to 'sh'. So, again, our letters and combination of letters are rough attempts to represent sounds-in-words.

Why 'rough'? For several reasons: it's not a regular system. Sometimes the letters represent different sounds – 'ough' even at the end of words can represent different sounds, as with 'enough', 'through', 'thorough', 'dough' and 'bough'. You can think of many others, of course, particularly with vowel letters and combinations of vowel letters. And there's another 'roughness': the same sound can be represented by different letters. In southern British pronunciation, the words 'saw', 'sore' and 'soar' are all pronounced the same way: different letters, same sound.

Another reason is more complicated. When we write, we spread letters out on the page evenly: with the same gaps between letters and the same gaps between words. Speech is not like that. We make long and short sounds as with, say, 'lute'. The 'oo' sound in the middle is longer than the 'l' and the 't' but visually or spatially such a difference is not repre-sented by how we space our letters. People with very good ears (or machines) can also hear how we 'flavour' or 'colour' pronunciations of one sound with the sound that comes before it or after it. In physical terms, as we're making one sound, we start to get our lips, tongue, teeth and breath ready to make the next sound! We alter the way we pronounce letters depending on nearby letter-sounds or the flow of speech, as with 'to' as 'tuh' or 'too'; 'sandwich' – 'samwich'; 'would you' – 'wuhjyou'; 'idea of' – 'idearof'; 'bet you' – 'betchyou'; 'cats and dogs' – 'cats'n'dogz'; 'train' – 'chrain' and many more.

Importantly, across the English-speaking world we also pronounce words very differently. All across the UK and Ireland we have many accents, and of course English is spoken as the native language or main language in scores of other countries. The letters then have what we might call 'different values'. People see the letters and in one place make one sound and in another place they make a different sound. There are hundreds of examples of this. Take the letters 'r' or 't'. Without much bother you can think of people in the English-speaking world who pronounce these very differently. Again, 'rough'. Or should we say rather that the sign 'r' indicates a variety of sounds that people make? It's not a limitless variety but it's quite wide nevertheless, as people use different parts of their mouths to make the sound.

Still with this, we also have a feature where seemingly important letters or 'signs' can be ignored! I speak southern British pronunciation. That means that when I say the words 'card' or 'mother' or 'four', I make sounds that are very different from how someone from the US or Scotland usually speaks. It would appear to some that I ignore the 'r', by saying 'cah-d' or 'moth-uh' or 'faw'. It follows then that when I read those letters-in-context, I make the letters do a job that's different from the job that an American or Scots person gets them to do, even though we arrive at the same word! How strange!

This reminds us of 'silent' letters – 'knock', 'write', 'right'. Many of these are historic survivals from a time when people did pronounce those words using sounds that the inventors of writing wanted to represent with letters. Nowadays we learn these (or not) as alternative ways of making the sound. We might say that, in context, 'kn' can be an 'n' sound and 'igh' can rhyme with 'eye' or 'I'. Does saying that make it easier to remember? Probably not. When we're writing, in order to distinguish 'write' from 'right' (easier than distinguishing 'right' from 'wrong'?!) depends on context, that's to say, how it falls in the sense of the phrase or passage – something I've learned since birth. I write, so, it's right to write (!).

Even so, and bearing all this in mind, what is this system? It's clearly different from the system used in hieroglyphs or traditional Chinese writing where signs represent words or parts of words in a pictorial way. The writing system you're looking at is based on the alphabet and combinations within that alphabet, as with 'th' or 'str' and so on. There is, then, an alphabetic principle involved. From a reader's point of view, we learn how to see letters-in-words and we make that overall sign (the word-in-context) mean something to us.

That 'word-in-context' phrase is very important. As you're reading this very sentence, your eye is moving to and fro, backwards and forwards in order to 'get it right', 'make it work', 'get the meaning' and so on. You're using your experience of talk, reading, writing and listening to do this. You're using your knowledge of the flow of English, your experience of reading, your sense of what things mean, your awareness of how English is put together – the order of words, the way we put phrases together, the kinds of sequences we use across many sentences and so on.

The moment we learn another language, much of this is thrown up into the air and we find ourselves arcing back to English and making comparisons. One example: in English we might write, 'I have eaten a good meal.' In German we would write (in effect): 'I have a good meal eaten.' As native speakers or people who are immersed in a language, this becomes embedded in our minds such that as we read, we read in context.

Other contexts that affect how we read are to do with the way we figure out the theme or topic of a piece. If we're reading about the sea, we bring our knowledge of sea-stuff, like 'waves' or 'ocean', to what we're reading. We also pick up on the type of writing it is – also called its 'genre'. If we think we're reading a newspaper article, an advert, a song lyric, instructions for self-constructed furniture, a road sign or a recipe, we bring expectations to the kind of language we're reading to help us 'get it'.

Now for some fun that demonstrates some of what I've been saying.

'The Chaos' (1922)
by Gerard Nolst Trenité

Dearest *creature* in *creation*
Studying English *pronunciation*,
    I will teach you in my *verse*
    Sounds like *corpse, corps, horse* and *worse.*

I will keep you, *Susy, busy,*
Make your *head* with *heat* grow dizzy;
    Tear in eye, your dress you'll *tear;*
    Queer, fair *seer, hear* my *prayer.*

Pray, console your loving *poet,*
Make my coat look *new,* dear, *sew it*!
    Just compare *heart, hear* and *heard,*
    Dies and *diet, lord* and *word.*

Sword and *sward, retain* and *Britain*
(Mind the latter how it's *written*).
    Made has not the sound of *bade,*
    Say – *said, pay* – *paid, laid* but *plaid.*

Now I surely will not *plague you*
With such words as *vague* and *ague,*
    But be careful how you *speak,*
    Say: *gush, bush, steak, streak, break, bleak,*

Previous, precious, fuchsia, via
Recipe, pipe, studding-sail, choir;
 Woven, oven, how and *low,*
 Script, receipt, shoe, poem, toe.

Say, expecting fraud and *trickery*:
Daughter, laughter and *Terpsichore,*
 Branch, ranch, measles, topsails, aisles,
 Missiles, similes, reviles.

Wholly, holly, signal, signing,
Same, examining, but *mining,*
 Scholar, vicar and *cigar,*
 Solar, mica, war and *far.*

From 'desire': *desirable – admirable* from 'admire',
Lumber, plumber, bier, but *brier,*
 Topsham, brougham, renown, but *known,*
 Knowledge, done, lone, gone, none, tone,

One, anemone, Balmoral,
Kitchen, lichen, laundry, laurel.
 Gertrude, German, wind and *wind,*
 Beau, kind, kindred, queue, mankind,

Tortoise, turquoise, chamois-leather,
Reading, Reading, heathen, heather.
 This phonetic labyrinth
 Gives *moss, gross, brook, brooch, ninth, plinth.*

Have you ever yet *endeavoured*
To pronounce *revered* and *severed,*
 Demon, lemon, ghoul, foul, soul,
 Peter, petrol and *patrol?*

Billet does not end like *ballet*;
Bouquet, wallet, mallet, chalet.
>*Blood* and *flood* are not like *food,*
>Nor is *mould* like *should* and *would.*

Banquet is not nearly *parquet,*
Which exactly rhymes with *khaki.*
>*Discount, viscount, load* and *broad,*
>*Toward,* to *forward,* to *reward,*

Ricocheted and *crocheting, croquet?*
Right! Your pronunciation's OK.
>*Rounded, wounded, grieve* and *sieve,*
>*Friend* and *fiend, alive* and *live.*

Is your R correct in *higher?*
Keats asserts it rhymes *Thalia.*
>*Hugh,* but *hug,* and *hood,* but *hoot,*
>*Buoyant, minute,* but *minute.*

Say *abscission* with *precision,*
Now: *position* and *transition;*
>Would it tally with my *rhyme*
>If I mentioned *paradigm?*

Twopence, threepence, tease are *easy,*
But *cease, crease, grease* and *greasy?*
>*Cornice, nice, valise, revise,*
>*Rabies,* but *lullabies.*

Of such puzzling words as *nauseous,*
Rhyming well with *cautious, tortious,*
>You'll *envelop* lists, I hope,
>In a linen *envelope.*

Would you like some more? You'll *have it!*
Affidavit, David, davit.
    To *abjure,* to *perjure. Sheik*
    Does not sound like *Czech* but *ache.*

Liberty, library, heave and *heaven,*
Rachel, loch, moustache, eleven.
    We say *hallowed,* but *allowed,*
    People, leopard, towed but *vowed.*

Mark the difference, moreover,
Between *mover, plover, Dover.*
    Leeches, breeches, wise, precise,
    Chalice, but *police* and *lice,*

Camel, constable, unstable,
Principle, disciple, label.
    Petal, penal, and *canal,*
    Wait, surmise, plait, promise, pal,

Suit, suite, ruin. Circuit, conduit
Rhyme with 'shirk it' and 'beyond it',
    But it is not hard to tell
    Why it's *pall, mall,* but *Pall Mall.*

Muscle, muscular, gaol, iron,
Timber, climber, bullion, lion,
    Worm and *storm, chaise, chaos, chair,*
    Senator, spectator, mayor,

Ivy, privy, famous; clamour
Has the A of *drachm* and *hammer.*
    Pussy, hussy and *possess,*
    Desert, but *desert, address.*

Golf, wolf, countenance, lieutenants
Hoist in *lieu* of flags left *pennants.*
 Courier, courtier, tomb, bomb, comb,
 Cow, but *Cowper, some* and *home.*

'*Solder, soldier*! Blood is *thicker*',
Quoth he, 'than *liqueur* or *liquor*',
 Making, it is sad but *true,*
 In bravado, much *ado.*

Stranger does not rhyme with *anger,*
Neither does *devour* with *clangour.*
 Pilot, pivot, gaunt, but *aunt,*
 Font, front, wont, want, grand and *grant.*

Arsenic, specific, scenic,
Relic, rhetoric, hygienic.
 Gooseberry, goose, and *close,* but *close,*
 Paradise, rise, rose, and *dose.*

Say *inveigh, neigh,* but *inveigle,*
Make the latter rhyme with *eagle.*
 Mind! *Meandering* but *mean,*
 Valentine and *magazine.*

And I bet you, dear, a *penny,*
You say *mani-*(fold) like *many,*
 Which is wrong. Say *rapier, pier,*
 Tier (one who ties), but *tier.*

Arch, archangel; pray, does *erring*
Rhyme with *herring* or with *stirring*?
 Prison, bison, treasure trove,
 Treason, hover, cover, cove,

Perseverance, severance. Ribald
Rhymes (but *piebald* doesn't) with *nibbled.*
>   *Phaeton, paean, gnat, ghat, gnaw,*
>   *Lien, psychic, shone, bone, pshaw.*

Don't be *down,* my *own,* but *rough it,*
And distinguish *buffet, buffet;*
>   *Brood, stood, roof, rook, school, wool, boon,*
>   *Worcester, Boleyn,* to *impugn.*

Say in sounds correct and *sterling*
Hearse, hear, hearken, year and *yearling.*
>   *Evil, devil, mezzotint,*
>   Mind the A! (A gentle hint.)

Now you need not pay attention
To such sounds as I don't mention,
>   Sounds like *pores, pause, pours* and *paws,*
>   Rhyming with the pronoun *yours;*

Nor are proper names *included,*
Though I often heard, as *you did,*
>   Funny rhymes to *unicorn,*
>   Yes, you know them, *Vaughan* and *Strachan.*

No, my maiden, coy and *comely,*
I don't want to speak of *Cholmondeley.*
>   No. Yet *Froude* compared with *proud*
>   Is no better than *McLeod.*

But mind *trivial* and *vial,*
Tripod, menial, denial,
>   *Troll* and *trolley, realm* and *ream,*
>   *Schedule, mischief, schism,* and *scheme.*

Argil, gill, Argyll, gill. Surely
May be made to rhyme with *Raleigh,*
    But you're not supposed to say
    Piquet rhymes with *sobriquet.*

Had this *invalid invalid*
Worthless documents? How *pallid,*
    How *uncouth* he, *couchant,* looked,
    When for *Portsmouth* I had booked!

Zeus, Thebes, Thales, Aphrodite,
Paramour, enamoured, flighty,
    Episodes, antipodes,
    Acquiesce, and *obsequies.*

Please don't monkey with the *geyser,*
Don't peel 'taters with my *razor,*
    Rather say in accents pure:
    Nature, stature and *mature.*

Pious, impious, limb, climb, glumly,
Worsted, worsted, crumbly, dumbly,
    Conquer, conquest, vase, phase, fan,
    Wan, sedan and *artisan.*

The Th will surely *trouble you*
More than R, Ch or W.
    Say then these phonetic *gems*:
    Thomas, thyme, Theresa, Thames.

Thompson, Chatham, Waltham, Streatham,
There are more but I *forget 'em—*
    Wait! I've got it: *Anthony,*
    Lighten your anxiety.

The archaic word *albeit*
Does not rhyme with *eight* – you *see it*;
    With and *forthwith*, one has voice,
    One has not, you make your choice.

Shoes, goes, does.* Now first say: *finger*;
Then say: *singer, ginger, linger.*
    Real, zeal, mauve, gauze and *gauge*,
    Marriage, foliage, mirage, age,

Hero, heron, query, very,
Parry, tarry, fury, bury,
    Dost, lost, post, and *doth, cloth, loth,*
    Job, Job, blossom, bosom, oath.

Faugh, oppugnant, keen *oppugners,*
Bowing, bowing, banjo-*tuners*
    Holm you know, but *noes, canoes,*
    Puisne, truism, use, to *use?*

Though the difference seems *little,*
We say *actual,* but *victual,*
    Seat, sweat, chaste, caste, Leigh, eight, height,
    Put, nut, granite, and *unite.*

Reefer does not rhyme with *deafer,*
Feoffer does, and *zephyr, heifer.*
    Dull, bull, Geoffrey, George, ate, late,
    Hint, pint, senate, but *sedate.*

Gaelic, Arabic, pacific,
Science, conscience, scientific;
    Tour, but *our, dour, succour, four,*
    Gas, alas, and *Arkansas.*

---

* No, you're wrong, this is the plural of *doe.*

Say *manoeuvre, yacht* and *vomit,*
Next *omit,* which differs from it
    Bona fide, alibi
    Gyrate, dowry and *awry.*

Sea, idea, guinea, area,
Psalm, Maria, but *malaria.*
    Youth, south, southern, cleanse and *clean,*
    Doctrine, turpentine, marine.

Compare *alien* with *Italian,*
Dandelion with *battalion,*
    Rally with *ally; yea, ye,*
    Eye, I, ay, aye, whey, key, quay!

Say *aver,* but *ever, fever,*
Neither, leisure, skein, receiver.
    Never guess – it is not *safe,*
    We say *calves, valves, half,* but *Ralf.*

Starry, granary, canary,
Crevice, but *device,* and *eyrie,*
    Face, but *preface,* then *grimace,*
    Phlegm, phlegmatic, ass, glass, bass.

Bass, large, target, gin, give, verging,
Ought, oust, joust, and *scour,* but *scourging;*
    Ear, but *earn;* and *ere* and *tear*
    Do not rhyme with *here* but *heir.*

Mind the O of *off* and *often*
Which may be pronounced as *orphan,*
    With the sound of *saw* and *sauce;*
    Also *soft, lost, cloth* and *cross.*

Pudding, puddle, putting. Putting?
Yes: at golf it rhymes with *shutting.*
> *Respite, spite, consent, resent.*
> *Liable,* but *Parliament.*

Seven is right, but so is *even,*
Hyphen, roughen, nephew, Stephen,
> *Monkey, donkey, clerk* and *jerk,*
> *Asp, grasp, wasp, demesne, cork, work.*

A of *valour, vapid vapour,*
S of *news* (compare *newspaper*),
> G of *gibbet, gibbon, gist,*
> I of *antichrist* and *grist,*

Differ like *diverse* and *divers,*
Rivers, strivers, shivers, fivers.
> *Once,* but *nonce, toll, doll,* but *roll,*
> *Polish, Polish, poll* and *poll.*

Pronunciation – think of *psyche!* –
Is a paling, stout and *spiky.*
> Won't it make you lose your *wits*
> Writing *groats* and saying 'grits'?

It's a dark *abyss* or *tunnel*
Strewn with stones like *rowlock, gunwale,*
> *Islington,* and *Isle* of *Wight,*
> *Housewife, verdict* and *indict.*

Don't you think so, reader, *rather,*
Saying *lather, bather, father?*
> Finally, which rhymes with *enough,*
> *Though, through, bough, cough, hough, sough, tough??*

Hiccough has the sound of *sup* …
My advice is: GIVE IT UP!

I used to think that I'd never be the kind of person who talks about the weather. The weather is just there. There really is no point in talking about it. You know what I do now? Talk about the weather. Why? And I only have the most banal and useless things to say about it like, 'It's really overcast, isn't it?' or 'Let's hope it'll clear up by the weekend.' People who wrote in had much, much better ones:

'My mum used to say "It's a monkey's wedding" if there was sunshine and rain at the same time. She can't remember where she got the phrase from.'

@jfeatherstonemc

'It's often larruping down in Yorkshire.'

@JimAturity

A great number of people recalled the following to describe bad weather:

– 'It's dark over Albert's mother's.'

– 'It's dark over our Bill's mother's.'

Where did these names come from, I wonder?

'My mum would always say about a blazing sun on a freezing cold day: "It's like a stepmother's smile – it shines but never warms."'

Norman Druker

A listener of *Word of Mouth*, Brian Williams, was eavesdropping on two elderly ladies on the bus. They were complaining about everything on the housing estate. They parted with one saying: 'Even the wind blows your hair.'

Brian says that the family has adopted it when overhearing similar conversations. 'One of us will turn to the other and say, "Even the wind blows your hair."'

For the rest of January, here are some more of the wonderful family sayings I've gathered from readers and listeners over the years:

'My grandad used to make up words for things that did not seem to have a name. He coined the word "spreezings" for the marks made on your skin when you lie on something like grass or blankets for a while. We all use the word in our family and one of us used it in an essay at school, thinking it was a commonly used term.'

Alison Sutton

'If you asked my mum the colour of something, she would invariably answer, "Sky-blue pink with a finny addy border" … I think "finny addy" could be a reference to smoked haddock, but I may be totally off the mark with that one!'

@DebMacc

'My mum always dried clothes inside on a "winter hedge", but she was the only person who ever used this word for a clothes horse.'

@LBashforth

'My grandmother and mother used to say, "Time is money to a weaver." Undoubtedly true but I have no idea why they said it.'

Sue Sparks

But is it poetry?

I often get asked this question and there is either no answer or a very long complicated one. So here goes:

For centuries it was an easy question to answer because poetry had rules – or, if you prefer the words, it had conventions, templates, blueprints or patterns. Poets used these templates for writing, such as employing lines with a certain rhythm or number of syllables, repeating sounds (as with Old English 'alliterative' poetry) and, of course, adopting rhyme schemes. These templates are a mix of music and maths. A great book on these is Stephen Fry's *The Ode Less Travelled*.

But writers are awkward people and they started experimenting. They asked: what if we're not so regular with the template? A writer like Walt Whitman (1819–1892) seems to have been inspired at least in part by the rhythms in the Bible and created poems with a similar feel to biblical prose. In fact, the 1611 King James Bible is remarkable for the kinds of rhythms and patterns contained within it, not least in the way in which the Psalms are laid out. It's one of my tongue-in-cheek provocations to say to people who object to non-rhyming poetry that 'free verse' has been around in English since the 1380s. John Wycliffe and colleagues produced a Bible that contains what are in effect 'prose poem' versions of what were once Hebrew songs – the Psalms. When the Geneva Bible of 1560 was produced, its authors produced a layout of the Psalms that is a kind of free verse. And as a consequence, they are all the more easy to recite. Most Bibles since then have of course followed suit. I've never heard anyone objecting to reading, reciting or singing 'The Lord's My Shepherd' on account of it not rhyming.

If you dig around, you can also find interesting experiments in how novelists wrote what we might call 'poetic prose'. One of the most famous of these is in Charles Dickens's *Bleak House* (1852–53):

Fog everywhere. Fog up the river, where it flows among green aits and meadows; fog down the river, where it rolls defiled among the tiers of shipping and the waterside pollutions of a great (and dirty) city. Fog on the Essex marshes, fog on the Kentish heights. Fog creeping into the cabooses of collier-brigs; fog lying out on the yards and hovering in the rigging of great ships; fog drooping on the gunwales of barges and small boats. Fog in the eyes and throats of ancient Greenwich pensioners, wheezing by the firesides of their wards; fog in the stem and bowl of the afternoon pipe of the wrathful skipper, down in his close cabin; fog cruelly pinching the toes and fingers of his shivering little 'prentice boy on deck. Chance people on the bridges peeping over the parapets into a nether sky of fog, with fog all round them, as if they were up in a balloon and hanging in the misty clouds ...

Try reading that out loud, hitting that word 'fog' as if it's a beat on a drum. You'll see, by the way, that Dickens has broken free of the demands of that rule: 'a sentence is a piece of writing that has a finite verb in it'. There's hardly a 'finite verb' in any of it! But is it a poem? Is it prose? What is it?

Even so, if you take the 50 or so years between 1870 and 1920, in that time writers all over the world experimented more than ever before with the shapes, rhythms and patterns of what they called poems, or sometimes, as with the French writer Baudelaire, 'prose poems'.

One of the most surprising came from W.E. Henley (1849–1903), an English poet who mostly wrote according to the templates. However, following a spell in hospital when his leg was amputated, he wrote a sequence of poems called 'In Hospital' (1888). The extreme situation seems to have given him the freedom to break the template and write like this:

Shoulders and loins
Ache – – – !
Ache, and the mattress,
Run into boulders and hummocks,
Glows like a kiln, while the bedclothes –

Tumbling, importunate, daft –
Ramble and roll, and the gas,
Screwed to its lowermost,
An inevitable atom of light,
Haunts, and a stentorous sleeper
Snores me to hate and despair.

[from 'Vigil']

By the time the Imagists were sharing their poems in the Café de la Tour Eiffel in Percy Street, London, in 1909, poets were consciously – self-consciously we might say – producing a 'new' kind of poem, both in shape and pattern but also in what and how a poet 'noticed'. Poems, they insisted, could look at small things in dispassionate ways.

Another area that 'allowed' or 'stimulated' writers to break from the conventions was through translations – as the Psalms had been. Rather than trying to squeeze the rhymes and rhythms of another language into English rhymes and rhythms, some writers (like Arthur Waley with Chinese poetry) created free verse poems. These traditions fed into how English-language poets wrote.

Since then, it's been a free-for-all. If two people get together and one person says, 'this is a poem' and the other person agrees, then who's to say, 'no it isn't'? We're not talking about the realm of law or science. This is the Republic of Letters!

Meanwhile, poets, readers and critics have noticed the influence on poetry of, say, blues, jazz, rock music, modernist music, rap, stand-up comedy and more. And partly arising out of the surrealist painters, people have experimented with 'shape poems' or 'concrete poetry'.

And let's not forget, no one has excluded all the old templates, or indeed prevented anyone from creating new templates using the methods laid down hundreds of years ago. The Poet Laureate Simon Armitage has translated the medieval poem *Sir Gawain and the Green Knight* in a way that reproduces much of the template of the original: old in new. Pam Ayres, John Cooper Clarke, Benjamin Zephaniah and Roger McGough have all produced work in traditional patterns or using traditional methods of rhythm and rhyme that have reached millions. There are styles of popular song – like grime – that are (to my ears) more like the old 'poetry-and-jazz' with its half-spoken, half-sung lyrics over music.

My view is that we can indeed be grumpy about 'modern poetry', though I've shown here that it's many hundreds of years old! Or we can think of it as a 'field of possibility'. We can read it without bothering too much whether it is or isn't poetry, and read it as 'stuff'. We can also think of it as a possibility for ourselves to write in any of the ways that others use or indeed to invent our own. Whether it's because we want to write 'to' someone, or 'about' something, or because we're in a state of despair, ecstasy or confusion, poetry offers us ways of talking on a page.

This act of composition slows down the stream of life or talk. It helps us reflect, contemplate and wonder. Once it's in front of us as a piece of writing, it enables us to check whether we're saying what we want to say. And of course we can change it in order to 'get it right'. All this can be a release and a relief. It can be fun. It can be dreamlike. It can be a way of being critical. It can be a way of saying 'here I am' or 'here we are'. The choice is ours.

One guiding principle I use – but this is not an instruc-tion – is to adopt the phrase that the poet W.H. Auden used: is it 'memorable speech'? There are many ways of making things memorable – using any of the old or new templates, or by creating phrases and images that are so striking, they last. Or both.

You may also want to adopt the principle of trying to make the familiar unfamiliar and the unfamiliar familiar. This may be through putting the 'best words in the best order'. It may be that you have a key guiding word in your mind, like 'irony' or 'absurd' or 'contrast' or 'flow' or 'figurative'. This last word carries within it the millions of times we all try to say that 'this' is like 'that' or that this represents something bigger than itself. That leaf falling from a tree represents something more than what it is … if we notice it and write about it.

So, to sum up: don't be grumpy, do it.

'My maternal "nana" in Cantley, Norfolk, had variations on "Sing at the table, die in the workhouse", "Read at the table, die in the workhouse", etc. We recite it still, re. mobile phones at the table, but only as a joke.'

@ABroadBrush

'When my nan couldn't hear what you said and wanted you to repeat it, she'd say, "Kill whose cat?"'

@Aliveandmasking

'When there was cause for celebration my dad would say, "Bugger the expense, buy the cat a goldfish." In other words, everybody is getting treated today.'

@DavidRisleyCPH

2 4

My own father would often say, 'What do you think this place is? Liberty Hall?' if he thought I was messing the place up or people were overstaying their welcome.

I've often wondered about it, so finally I looked it up. The Oxford Reference online says:

> Liberty Hall: a place where one may do as one likes. The phrase comes originally from Oliver Goldsmith's *She Stoops to Conquer* (1773).

2 5

'Whenever there's too much of something, e.g. bread, my mother uses the phrase: "There's enough bread to cobble dogs!" I use it now whenever there's a surfeit of something.'

@AndrewSylvesr

2 6

As some of my readers might know, my father was an Arsenal fan, but he always called them 'dem bums' – American, of course, but I gather it's what fans of the Brooklyn Dodgers call the team. He must have picked up the phrase in the US Army.

2 7

Holocaust Memorial Day

This is the day on which people can remember the catastrophe that befell the Jewish people between 1933 and 1945 at the hands of the Nazis and their collaborators. The events that mark the day are also opportunities to remember the terror, massacres, mass killings and incarcerations that happened to others whom the Nazis designated as 'Unter-menschen' – literally 'under-people' but which we translate as 'sub-human', such as the so-called congenitally mentally or physically deficient, 'Gypsies' (more properly called Roma and Sinti these days), non-Jewish Poles, Jehovah's Witnesses, gay men, people of colour, and civilians in occupied countries in places like Oradour-sur-Glane and Lidice.

What to call something as immense as this is not with-out problems. The word Holocaust itself was coined from a Greek word meaning 'burnt offering'. It perhaps goes with-out saying that some people have objected to this precisely because what happened was by no means an 'offering' and though cremation was one part of the genocides, not all victims were burnt. There is also debate as to whether the word 'Holocaust' refers to all civilian victims of the Nazis or specifically to the Jewish victims. You can find books and papers using the word in either sense.

The word 'Shoah' is Hebrew and translates as 'catastro-phe' and there are Shoah memorials and foundations. I go to the Mémorial de la Shoah in Paris because that's where my father's uncles and aunt are commemorated.

In this book, I've tried to focus on the fact that we make language in the situations we live in and through. I researched the fate of my family in the Second World War and I realised that my father's uncles and aunts spoke several languages: Yiddish, Polish, French and German. My father's uncle Oscar (aka Jeschie), who spoke Polish, Yiddish and French, wrote to his brother in the US in perfect German. Even so, the main shared language of that generation in my family was Yiddish. The Yiddish word for the Holocaust is 'khurbn', meaning 'destruction', though it's what linguists would call a loan word from Hebrew.

When I think about this, it reminds me of something that has slipped out of view: the majority of Jews killed in the Holocaust/Shoah/khurbn spoke Yiddish. This is by no means to neglect or exclude people who spoke other languages. Rather, it makes me ask about what languages do I hear or read when finding out about these events? Nearly always English, sometimes French, sometimes German. I hardly ever hear or read about it in Yiddish. But nearly all history used to be like this: events told by historians about others, with hardly any use of the words that the ordinary people spoke or wrote at the time. This has changed hugely in the last 30 years or more – think of the archives of people's experiences of wars.

These thoughts about the fact that I don't 'know' the Holocaust in the language of my relatives (the language of the majority of the Jewish victims) was one of the reasons I started to study Yiddish.

The other reason I wanted to learn Yiddish is that I wanted to join the dots between the 'dots' that my parents and grand-parents spoke. In fact, before we started the classes, we were asked to give some sense of how much Yiddish we already knew. I sat down with a piece of paper and thought myself back to scenes from my home life 60 and 70 years earlier. If you're someone whose parents spoke a language other than English, you'll understand what I'm about to talk about here. By the time I had finished scribbling it came to something like 300 words and expressions.

My parents used Yiddish in fits and starts, as a way of expressing things that they must have felt they couldn't put into words in English as precisely or with as much feeling as they could in Yiddish. As a child and teenager, I absorbed this as part of who we were without thinking clearly about it.

Let's start with a chicken. Chicken was a big deal back in the 1950s. It was something you had once a week at most. The massive proliferation of KFC, chicken curry, super-market packs of diced chicken, chicken legs, chicken thighs, chicken wings, chicken soup, chicken with everything, hadn't happened.

In my mind, a roast chicken on the table even now trans-lates itself into 1950s home Yiddish: I see my father saying, 'Who wants the pulke?' (the leg), the 'fliegel' (the wing), the 'heene shmalts' (chicken fat) that must be saved, and long eulogies about his bubbe's chicken soup full of 'lokshn' (pasta) or 'kneydlekh' (dumplings). In fact, though it's absolute taboo to say it, I don't think my mother's chicken soup was very good! May I be cursed forever for saying so.

When I look at my list of 300 words and expressions, I can see that many of the words are ways of describing people and sentiments. Every language has these but the reason my parents used them and that I remember them is because they must have felt they fitted the situation at that moment, with more edge or piquancy than English.

Do you know the Mr Men books? It occurred to me that I could create Mr Mensh books. A 'mensh' in Yiddish means a good person. Each Mr Mensh book could be one of the people or sentiments that my parents talked about:

- Mr Shlump – the guy who walks about in clothes he's been wearing all week

- Mr Shlokh – the guy who walks about in clothes he's been wearing all year

- Mr Momzah – the guy who you don't want to know

- Mr Shpilkes – the guy who's always worried

- Mr Dreck – the guy who's crap

- Mr Nebbish – the guy who looks like he's turned everything into crap

- Mr Farkakte – the guy who looks like he's crapped himself

- Mr Bubkes – the guy who talks crap

- Mr Pisher – another guy who is crap

- Mr Bubbele – the guy who is so much of a mummy's boy he's a grandmother's boy

- Mr Shmerel – the guy who's a bit of a fool

- Mr Shlemiel – the other guy who's a bit of a fool

- Mr Shmendrik – another guy who's a bit of fool

- Mr Kvell – the guy who's very proud of his son for having made some soup

- Mr Kvetch – the guy who moans about the soup

- Mr Chup – the guy who slurps the soup

- Mr Shmalts – the guy who's dribbled the soup down his front

- Mr Shnorrer – the guy who wants your soup

- Mr Chap – the guy who grabs your soup

- Mr Khazze – the guy who can't stop having soup

- Mr Shmooze – the guy who sweet-talks you to get your soup off you

- Mr Zhuzh – the guy who can turn a lousy soup into a good soup

- Mr Knakke – the guy who thinks he knows more than everyone else about how to make soup

- Mr Meshuggeh – the guy who talks nonsense about the soup

- Mr Kibbits – the guy who wants to have a chat while you're having the soup

- Mr Yakhne – the guy who can't stop talking about the soup

- Mr Gantse Megillah – the guy who talks about every single thing that's in the soup

- Mr Bochur – the guy who's reading a book about the soup

- Mr Gubba – the guy who tells you how to make the soup

- Mr Ganuf – the guy who nicks your soup

- Mr Shtum – the guy who keeps quiet about the guy who nicked your soup

- Mr Kishkes – the guy who says that soup gives him a bellyache

- Mr Greps – the guy who has his soup and burps

–

– Mr Fotz – the guy who has his soup and farts

– Mr Gantse Makher – the guy who owns the soup factory

Since I've been, let's say, ten years old, there are hardly any bits of writing in modern English that I can't read to myself, even if I don't understand them. The ones I don't understand are the ones where I 'bark at print'. I make mostly the right noises (either in my head or out loud) whether I understand it or not. If you're reading this (as opposed to listening to it on audio) then you're in the same shoes as me. Now imagine you're in a class and in front of you is a text written in a writing system you don't know. Perhaps you know this situation because you've learned Greek, Russian, Arabic, Mandarin or any other language that uses systems different from the one you're reading now. If you don't know what this feels like, I can tell you it's like groping round a room when there's a power cut.

This is what has happened to me (in fact it's entirely self-inflicted) by learning Yiddish. That's because though Yiddish can be written with 'Roman' letters (as I did with my Mr Mensh piece), it is traditionally – some would say properly – written with Hebrew letters. One small example: a word that sounds like the German word for 'I' – in German 'ich' – is written איך.

To give you some idea of why that's just a little bit hard for a newbie: first, read from right to left; then the first letter is the beautiful 'shtumer alef', a letter that is always silent (shtum), and is there to indicate that the next letter is a vowel; then the second letter is a 'yud' and that gives you the 'i' sound; and then there's the last letter. Ah yes, the last letter which is sometimes a last-letter letter, if you get me. Some of the letters have two forms: one for when they are at the end of a word, and the other when they're elsewhere in a word. That last letter in אין is a 'lange khof', telling you that there is another 'khof' out there. Now you can read 'ikh', and you'll see I've written that 'transliterated' into Roman letters.

Are you still with me?

Ah, you might be thinking, but surely Michael learned Hebrew letters when he was a boy going to Hebrew classes called 'cheder' or 'kheyder'. Well, my secular parents didn't enrol me into Hebrew classes but when I was seven a boy came up to me in the playground and said, 'You are, aren't you?'

'What?' I said.

'Jewish,' he said.

'I think so,' I said.

'My mum says that you should come to Hebrew classes,' he said. 'They're every Sunday in the synagogue in the old Methodist chapel and Mum is the teacher.'

So that night I went home and said, 'A boy at school called Peter says that I should go to Hebrew classes.'

And my mum said, 'That's nice,' so off I went.

But ...

... we went on a Hebrew class outing to Chessington Zoo, and I wandered off on my own. When I came back to the rendezvous point, everyone was very cross with me.

'Where have you been? What have you been doing?'

I said, 'I thought you said we could all go off where we want.'

'That was in your group,' they said. They made the word 'group' sound slightly threatening. 'You were supposed to be in your groooop. We've spent the whole afternoon looking for you.'

I sat on the bus on the way home feeling bad. I had spoiled everyone's trip to Chessington Zoo.

So I said to Mum, 'I'm not going to Hebrew class any more.' And she said, 'Alright then.'

This adds up to one simple truth: I only got as far as learning three letters: aleph, gimel and vov.

When I started my first Yiddish class and looked at the letters they were entirely intertwined with Peter, his mum (who incidentally I thought was stunningly beautiful from the point of view of a seven-year-old boy) and being bad at Chessington Zoo.

It's interesting, isn't it, how learning something is never just a matter of learning. The learning is intertwined with 'stuff'.

Anyway, I'm slow but I'm doing OK but I have to accept the fact that I can't do what I do when I look at a page of English writing – which is to scan it at fantastic speed getting the drift of what it's about. Sometimes I recognise whole words, but a lot of the time, I'm plodding along, letter by letter. It's a humbling experience for a 78-year-old.

In the speech he gave when he accepted his Nobel Prize, the writer Isaac Bashevis Singer said:

> People ask me often, 'Why do you write in a dying language?' And I want to explain it in a few words.
>
> Firstly, I like to write ghost stories and nothing fits a ghost better than a dying language. The deader the language the more alive is the ghost. Ghosts love Yiddish and as far as I know, they all speak it.
>
> Secondly, not only do I believe in ghosts, but also in resurrection. I am sure that millions of Yiddish-speaking

corpses will rise from their graves one day and their first question will be: 'Is there any new Yiddish book to read?' For them Yiddish will not be dead.

I don't have to agree with Isaac Bashevis Singer, but I do know that one of the reasons why I am learning Yiddish is so that in some way I can be amongst the people I have found on my family tree – ghosts in their own way, I guess. I want to know the words they used to describe their journeys, their worries, their loves and their losses. I can say in English, 'Morris Rosen left his home in Krośniewice to come to London …' but what does it feel like to say that in his language? What does it feel like to be able to read the poems and stories he read or sing the songs he sang?

As a first thought, I confess that this is weird. And yet I'm someone who spent many hours in school studying Latin and many hours at university studying Old English, either or both of which studies are justified in terms of 'our roots' or 'the roots of our language' or 'getting to know where we came from; how our ancestors thought'.

Yes indeed.

It is genuinely amazing to read what Julius Caesar or Catullus wrote in their own words. It is thrilling to read the words about the grim and greedy monster Grendel in *Beowulf* or the wit of the Old English riddles. I don't regret a minute of it. All I'm doing then, I say to myself, is extending that expression 'our roots' to encompass my family roots.

And do you know, there are times when our Yiddish teacher speaks, I hear an expression that my parents used and I tingle. I have a physical feeling that connects me to my mother and father as if they are there. 'Sei a mensh,' our teacher says. 'Sei a mensh,' my father says to me from 70 years earlier, 'and nip to the shops for me, will you?' ('Be a good person and …')

Every time you say the word February, you are invoking the idea of purifying yourself. The month owes its name to the Latin word 'februum', which means 'purification' – though within the word is the idea of warming and heating. Our word 'fever' is related. The Februa (the plural of 'februum') are the purifications or purgings, and Februa (or Februatus) was the name of a festival held in Rome on 15 February. The goddess Juno was also invoked here because she was sometimes known as Juno Februalis. As you might guess, Juno gets another look-in, when we get to June.

Now, if you were an ancient Roman, how did you do your purgings? You headed to the Lupercal cave on Palatine Hill and took part in a festival. This involved the sacrifice of a goat and a dog and some smearing of blood. This was to honour Rumina, the goddess of breastfeeding, and a nearby wild fig tree where Romulus and Remus (the founders of Rome) were once taken. You'll remember that Romulus and Remus were suckled by a wolf.

The fig tree is a crucial part of this because it was called 'capricus' (literally 'goat-fig') and what with figs being thought to resemble breasts and the tree having a milk-like sap, the connection between figs, milk and goats was made.

Later this festival became known as the Lupercalia or Lupercal.

For the act of naming February, we should thank Numa Pompilius. Until he came along, the Romans had thought of winter as being monthless. Winter is 'less' of a lot of things in the Northern Hemisphere but it feels odd to think of it as having no months, though hibernating animals can take it in one long uninterrupted stretch if it stays cold enough.

So who was Numa Pompilius – another ingredient of February lying hidden behind the word? He was the second king of Rome, living from around 753 to 672 BC and much praised for being wise and pious. It's said that he wrote several sacred books and asked for these to be buried with him when he died. Some 500 years later, an act of nature revealed what was inside the tomb. The books were inspected by the authorities who decided that they were inappropriate for all to see. They were duly burned. There's an alternative twist to this part of the story: some said that the high priests (the 'pontifices') took them and kept them for themselves – a strange echo of some people's experience of school, when inappropriate books, comics and magazines were seized by teachers and never returned.

This brings a note to February of book-burning or hoarding of dubious material, which seems a far cry from purification.

Before English speakers took on the word February, they talked of this time as 'kale-monath' – cabbage-month – or 'solmonath', which originally people thought meant mud-month but is now thought to mean 'hearth-cake month'. This refers to festive cakes that were eaten and, according to the Venerable Bede (672–735), offered to the gods.

You can see why people describe Old English as 'earthy'.

When I asked people about their favourite family sayings, I really didn't imagine I'd find so many answers to the question 'What's for dinner?' In this month are a few of my favourites.

'"What's for tea?" was "a rasher of wind and a fried snowball".'

@kathy_pimlott

'My grandfather was the only person I know who still used the term "orts" to mean leftovers (as in Shakespeare's "abjects, orts and imitations"). Wirral, Merseyside, 1960s.'

Sue Millard

'My grandma, herself a dry-humoured Hull lass, used to respond to the question of "What's for tea?" with the regular response of "Shit with sugar on!"'

@CheKaye

'If my mum was ever asked, "What's for tea?" the stock Lancastrian reply was, "Th' oven door, buttered …"'

@DGSetchell

'"What's for tea, Mum?" "Bees' knees and flies' elbows."'

@cherry_red186

'If asked what was for dinner, my grandad would say, "Cheese and pump handles" or "Windmill pie. If it goes round, you might get some."'

@Silo1978

'The reply to "What's for lunch?" from my mum would often be "Bread and clap it" – I always imagined bread clapped together with whatever could be found. Asking "What's for pudding?" got the response "Wait and see."'

@guineagibbs

'"What's for tea?" "Two chunks of the cupboard door and a bite of the knob."'

@timcurtisart

'In answer to my plaintive squeak, "What's for tea?" my mum would say either "Chopped straw and buttermilk" or "Hot spiced cake and walk slow". It was what her father Ambrose Rigley from County Wexford used to say to her!"'

Deb Klemperer

'"What's for dinner?" "Three jumps at the pantry door."'

@Gemski_b

'"What's for dinner?" Dad would reply, "The same as yesterday but a little bit less." And give a hearty chuckle.'

@siandeller

As Valentine's Day is approaching, it's time for a quote. The author of *The Little Prince* was (let's enjoy his full name) Antoine Marie Jean-Baptiste Roger, Comte de Saint-Exupéry. Something with the beauty of simplicity from him: 'Love is not just looking at each other, it's looking in the same direction.' From *Wind, Sand and Stars*.

Valentine's Day

Valentine's Day is of course a day in honour of St Valentine, who is, amongst other things, the patron saint of epilepsy and beekeepers. If you would like to take a romantic trip in celebration of today, you could visit Rome and the Basilica of Santa Maria in Cosmedin, where you'll find exhibited there Valentine's skull crowned with flowers. However, a little research on Valentine's relics and you will see that they can be found in at least ten churches across Europe.

St Valentine was a Christian martyr – that's to say he was martyred for being a Christian, which happened on 14 February AD 269.

1950s decency could be maintained with this:

I love you, I love you, I love you, so mighty.
I wish your pyjamas were next to my nightie.
Don't be mistaken, don't be misled,
I mean on the washing line and not in bed.

If today is going to be your day for telling someone you like them, this one may work: 'Hey, my name's Microsoft. Can I crash at your place tonight?'

Maybe not.

The 'roses are red' formula is useful. Make your own along these lines:

Roses are red
Violets are blue
You're the reason I'm smiling
– That and chocolate fondue.

The day after Valentine's Day. Just in case it's a downer, this may help:

Roses are red
Violets are blue
Most poems rhyme
This one doesn't.

Similes are one kind of 'figure of speech' or 'figurative language' along with metaphors and personification. We are fascinated by the idea that something can be like something else. Even a seemingly objective expression like 'electric current' owes its origins to the figurative idea that scientists believed that electricity flowed through wires like a current of water, the word 'current' holding within it the idea of running, as with 'coursing'.

When we do this obviously in an upfront sort of a way, they are known as similes, a word that means 'like' in Latin. We can do this with the word 'like' but also with 'as' or even in constructions like, 'You're more suspicious than …' or 'I'm as hungry as a …'

The TV series *Blackadder* specialised in similes:

> Baldrick: 'I have a plan, sir.'
> Blackadder: 'Really, Baldrick? A cunning and subtle one?'
> Baldrick: 'Yes, sir.'
> Blackadder: 'As cunning as a fox who's just been appointed Professor of Cunning at Oxford University?'

When I asked people for family sayings, many of these included similes.

A popular one – this means standing there not knowing what you're doing or why: 'You're standing there like piffy on a rock bun.'

There's been some discussion on the meaning of 'piffy', with some saying that it means icing sugar. Some say it means raisins.

'My mum says, "You shape like one of Lewis's", meaning that we're as useless as the mannequins in Lewis's department store in Liverpool which no longer exists.'

@redgierob

'Stood there like one of Lewis's = stood doing nothing.'

@sharn46

'Nan, a Londoner, would say if someone was restless: "Sit down, you're like a fart in a colander."'

@Rosindell1

My own dad Harold would say in similar circumstances, 'I've been running around like a fart in a bottle.'

'I have a friend who once pointed across the room and declared some famous person as "mad as that chair". "Mad as a chair" has been my go-to term to describe anyone given to crazy actions or pronouncements ever since.'

@katedavispoet

'My aunt said of someone constantly in and out of prison: "He was in and out like a fiddler's elbow."'

@Patfergusontoo

'My grandma (born 1905) used to refer to precocious children (self included) as being "as fly as a box of monkeys".'

@Rigsbyhatstand

'From Dad: "Look at the state of him, dressed up like a pox doctor's clerk."'

@kevinmitchell50

'My manager at an animal rescue centre liked to describe disgruntled people as having "a face like a torn scone". That was civilised Edinburgh. The Glasgow version is "a face like a well-skelped [beaten] arse".'

@PhdTownTrail

'He's got a face like a torn melodeon.'

[Several sources]

'My father would describe someone who was exceptionally well dressed as "flash as a rat with a gold tooth".'

@faustajj

'I've heard someone be described as "so lazy his skin wouldn't graft".'

@Chris555Tompa

William Archibald Spooner (1844–1930) was a clergyman and 'don' (tutor) at Oxford University. He had the reputation of being absent-minded and delivering the muddle we now call 'spoonerisms', swapping part of one word with another. There are very few of these that are definitely his and the ones that are agreed to be his are mostly the least funny, as with 'The weight of rages will press hard upon the employer' (rate of wages). (I did warn you about it not being funny.)

Others that may or may not be Spooner's own spooner-isms are:

— 'It is kisstomary to cuss the bride.'

— 'You have tasted two worms.'

— 'You will leave by the next town drain.'

You can of course make up your own. A feminist theatre company in the 1970s called themselves 'Cunning Stunts'.

People sent in some as family sayings:

'Dum and Mad, mangers and bash, acon and beggs, crustard and mess.'

@ThroughTheGaps

'We were teasing my mother once when she shouted, "You're all futterly owl!"'

@Rose73526444

Another favourite many people sent in was 'chish and fips'.

'My grandmother was a real one for spoonerisms; my favour-ite one that I use to this day is "two-play wug" (two-way plug).'

@linguistforsail

March

March is one of the months of the year that offers scope for puns as there are alternative meanings for the word, but as with January and February we should look back instead to the Romans to explain the origins of its name. It comes from 'Martius', which in turn came from the god Mars. He was the god of war and farming, a pairing which we, in the modern world, might almost regard as opposites. Not to the Romans, who were able to view the onset of battle and the onset of ploughing and sowing as similar.

The Romans could also think of Mars as being their ancestor, as he was the father of the founders of Rome, Romulus and Remus. If Mars is starting to coalesce in your mind as some kind of alpha male figure, you would be right. We might view him through Roman eyes as representing the life force. He could help make crops grow and ward off natural catastrophes that might harm them. It was said, for example, that if you devoted yourself properly to Mars, he could fend off the kind of blight and disease that affects wheat. Mars – like his Norse equivalent Thor – was also, at some point in the Roman era, connected to thunder.

Though March in Roman times was full of festivals, Mars himself was not a focal point for all of them. That said, one ritual that started on 1 March and carried on through the month called on one sect of priests, the Salii, to perform important tasks. The Salii were the 'jumping priests' – jumping in the air being a task that was thought to help the crops grow, perhaps through sympathetic magic, imitating the action of crops growing upwards in order to induce it to happen. In March, the Salii were also called upon to parade the 12 sacred shields that were kept in the Temple of Mars.

One of these shields was divine because it had fallen from heaven, sent by Jupiter to Numa Pompilius (who we met in February). Clever Numa ordered 11 copies to be made in order to confuse would-be thieves. After all, it was thought that the original shield helped secure Rome's presence and future.

So one way to think of March is to bring to mind 12 high priests wearing embroidered tunics under purple cloaks, sporting garlands of white ribbons, conical caps and wheat sheaves. They are parading the sacred shields, beating them with sticks or daggers, performing dances, leaping into the air, singing the *Carmen Saliare*, a fragment of which goes:

> O Planter God, arise. Everything indeed have I committed
> unto (thee as) the Opener. Now art thou the Doorkeeper,
> thou art the Good Creator, the Good God of Beginnings.

The first English word for March, incidentally, commemorated someone else altogether, a goddess known in modern English as Rheda. She is mentioned in the Venerable Bede's work *The Reckoning of Time* (*De temporum ratione*) but he says little else about Rheda apart from the fact that people sacrificed something in her honour.

What or who was sacrificed, we can only guess.

St David's Day

St David was born in 500 and died on 1 March – St David's Day – in 589. He is the only native-born patron saint of the countries of Britain and Ireland. His mother, St Non, gave birth to him during a storm on a Pembrokeshire clifftop. The ruins of Non's chapel mark the spot. It's said that David lived off leeks and water.

While we're on leeks, the famous music hall star, Marie Lloyd, born in Hoxton, London, in 1870, sang a song with the line: 'I sits among the cabbages and peas.' Some eagle-eyed spotters of double entendres objected to the vulgarity. Marie Lloyd was happy to make the line decent with: 'I sits among the cabbages and leeks.'

Some advice from St David: 'Gwnewch y pethau bychain mewn bywyd.' Meaning: 'Do the little things in life.'

'My dad always called dusk "dumpsey light" and he always said it was his father's term for it. They were from Gloucester.'

Sarah Daly

St Piran's Day

St Piran is a holy man of Cornwall and so is the patron saint of tinners. I don't think my mother was celebrating him when she stacked the larder in our house with scores of corned beef tins. When there was the typhoid scare of 1964, which was thought to have been caused by corned beef imported from South America, my mother went to the cupboard, took down a tin of corned beef and said, 'Better not open that till the typhoid outbreak is over.'

Back with St Piran. He seems to have been what the guide-books call 'the merriest, hardest-drinking, hardest-living holy man Cornwall ever knew', according to the Cornwall Heritage Trust. His feast day used to be kept as a holiday in the parishes of Perranzabuloe (meaning 'Piran in the sand'), St Agnes and St Day, and others where tin mining has always been the main occupation.

When you're drinking to St Piran, you should say 'Yeghes da!' (pronounced 'yecki-da'), meaning 'good health' in Cornish.

Cornish (Kernewek or Kernowek) is what is described as a 'Southwestern Brittonic language of the Celtic language family'. It derives from Common Brittonic, an extinct language spoken throughout much of Great Britain before English came to dominate. Welsh and Breton also come from this root.

The Cornish language can be (and is) studied, learned, read, written and spoken, and it survives both with individual words and expressions but also in the way that many Cornish people speak English. This is what's known as the 'substrate' phenomenon. That's to say, the old or previous language spoken by a group of people can be 'heard' in the way in which the more recent language is spoken. (With Yiddish and English we call it 'Yinglish'.) One example would be to talk of 'March month'.

Some Cornish dialect words for you: aglets – hawthorn berries; betwattled – confused; and one I have to include: buzza or bussa – a large salting pot or bread-bin, also found in the phrase 'dafter than a buzza'.

Why do I have to include it? Because my PE teacher at school (1962–64) was a Cornishman called … Mr Buzza.

If only I had known 'dafter than a buzza'.

A story for you.

For several years, Piran advised a certain King Aengus (in Ireland). Aengus grew tired of his wife and became enamoured of a lady of the court who he thought was younger and more beautiful. Piran felt that it was his duty to forbid this so he preached against the king in front of the whole court. Aengus was none too pleased about this so he condemned Piran to be bound to a millstone and thrown off the highest cliff in Munster.

On a cold winter's day Piran was bound to a heavy granite stone and thrown off the cliff. When the stone hit the sea far below, the ropes binding Piran became loose and the stone floated.

It sailed with Piran all the way to the north coast of Cornwall, at which point he realised that God was telling him to teach the Gospel to the Cornish people, who until then had worshipped their own Celtic gods of the sun and rain. Piran built himself a little church, which to this day still stands near Perranporth: St Piran's Oratory. It is said to be the oldest Christian church in Britain.

A Twitter follower writes:

'My great-aunt (born 1888) who lived with us when I was a child used to say to me (when I was being a nuisance), "Tha'd mither a boat horse till it dropt in t' cut."'

@Megthelibraria1

A response in the comments explained it was a canal reference – the horse falling in the cut (canal) because it got distracted.

And another:

'I had a grandfather who had a very whimsical turn of phrase for many things. One that comes to mind is his description of mopeds as "bees in a bottle".'

@ArdPad

Words in context

I want you to imagine the word 'stop'. Actually it's in capital letters: STOP. Think where you might see this word and what it might mean.

It could be on some kind of post indicating that buses or coaches will stop there. That means it would be a noun. Usually you can put the word 'a' or 'the' in front of a noun. Usually you can have more than one of them, so you can make the singular 'a stop' or 'the stop' into the plural 'stops', 'the stops' and 'some stops'. Some plurals can sound odd though: 'happinesses' or 'geographies' – possible but odd. And if you have a singular noun that already sounds plural, like 'economics' or 'politics', it's hard (impossible?) to make it more plural by saying 'economicses', so we end up saying things like 'different types of economics'. So that's a little exploration into whether my STOP sign was a noun.

But what if this STOP is a sign by the side of the road that you can see from your car? This is different. It's an order or command. The sign is telling you to stop driving and come to a halt. That's a kind of verb. Grammarians are people who give names to different kinds of verb. They call this kind an 'imperative'. You use these all day long: 'Hand me that screw-driver', 'Eat up, kids'.

But what if this STOP isn't either of these? A bit more information: it's engraved onto a red button on a bus. Is it a noun, telling us that this button is a stop, a place where something or other will stop? No. Is it telling you to stop? No. So what is it? It's a sign telling you that if you press the button, the driver will get a signal telling them that they should stop the bus at the next 'bus stop'.

If you're like me, you know this. You see it, you want to get off, you press the button. How do you know this? Most probably because you've seen other people pressing it, you possibly heard a noise, saw a sign that flashes 'bus stopping' and the driver stopped the bus. Result! That's how you 'got' it. The experience of watching and hearing has told you how to read this STOP. Yes, you could read it in the sense of being able to make the sounds that make up the word; in fact you probably already knew the word from other situations. But without the specific knowledge and context, you wouldn't know if this STOP was the noun meaning that this is some kind of place where things stop or the verb that is a command telling you to stop. Or, as in this case, neither of these.

Why does this matter? It matters because you have 'got' the meaning of STOP from its context, a context that you have learned over time. Context and our knowledge-history are crucial to how we understand the language being used around us all day long, every day.

If this STOP isn't a noun or verb, what should we call it, given that it isn't doing what nouns or verbs do? And it doesn't even really mean 'stop' in the sense we usually use it to mean. This STOP means: 'If you press me, a signal will reach the bus driver who will make the bus stop.' What if there isn't actually a term (of the same kind as 'noun' or 'verb') to describe this?

To help us here, we might have to look around and see if this STOP is unique or found in other places too. On my computer I have the sign 'option'. It's written on one of the keys on my keyboard. Strangely, it's not offering me an option (noun) nor is it telling me to option something (verb). It's saying: 'If you press this button at the same time as you press another key, you will be able to print a letter or sign that is not shown on the keyboard keys.' In fact, it's not really any more of an option than anything else on the keyboard, because every key is also really an option, and the shift button offers yet another kind of option.

So in a way the STOP sign and the 'option' key are quite similar. What shall we call this then? An 'if-you-press-me'? Or what?

The account I've just given tells us a lot about words, language, grammar and grammatical terms and how we make meaning from context and history of context. It also tells us that there could be gaps in the naming systems that grammarians have invented. But how could that be? Grammarians have been describing languages for thousands of years. Surely there are no gaps left?

Now let's go in a bit deeper.

I was listening to Radio 4 and someone said, 'I'm really bad at grammar.'

I thought, really? Here was a woman, speaking fluently and cleverly, so how could she be 'bad at grammar'? What did she mean? I guess she meant that she wasn't very good at remembering grammar terminology or, perhaps, when she was at school, she didn't do very well at grammar exercises, whether that was in English or in lessons on other languages. All this suggests to me a confusion about how we use the word 'grammar'.

Let me try an analogy: the human body. If you're alive while you're reading this (!), you're good at 'having a body'. A whole set of systems is working – heart, lungs, nerves, organs. However, you may be 'bad at anatomy' – that is you can't remember the names of parts of your body. Even more, you may be bad at physiology, i.e. bad at remembering what different parts of your body do. So you can be good at having a body but be bad at knowing words about your body, and the functions of your body.

Same goes for grammar. If you're reading (or hearing this) and you're understanding this, you're brilliant at grammar. You may or may not know many of the terms about the language that you're understanding and using, though. This tells us that we need two phrases: 'grammar use' and 'grammar terms'.

I think 'grammar use' doesn't get much of a good press – or hardly any press at all. It's an invisible knowledge that most of us are very good at. What's incredible about it is that we learn most of it by the time we are five. Perhaps that's why we don't rate it. After all, in the general run of praising people for being brilliant, we don't usually include what nought-to-five-year-olds do. There are of course books on language acquisition but they tend to be for specialists. We much prefer to hear stories about children *not* being able to speak these days (apparently).

Now let's look for a moment at 'grammar terms'. I know that this bores some people to tears, though there are others who are thrilled at the way in which grammar terms seem to be able to dissect and name language as accurately as anatomists can name the muscles of the neck. Here are some grammar terms to do with naming kinds of words: noun, verb, adjective, adverb, conjunction, preposition. Here are some terms to do with parts of words: stem, prefix, suffix, inflection. Here are some to do with structures: sentence, clause, phrase. Here are some grammar terms to do with the function of words: subject, object. Grammarians go on to name, for example, types of these as with some types of verb or different forms of a verb. Likewise for example different kinds of sentences, or different kinds of clauses, and so on through much of these terms. This makes for there being a long (very long!) and complex set of grammar terms. What's more, some of these terms vary or die out. One example of many: when I was at school, there was one kind of verb that we were told was called 'present continuous'. Primary school children in England are now told it's the 'present progressive'. There are examples of the same word usage having different names, depending on which book you're reading or who's teaching you.

So sticking with the human body analogy, I'll now set up a problem. Do you think that the terms we come up with for the human body should *describe* what bodies are actually like or should they tell what *ideal* human bodies should be like? Here's an example: skin colour. Medical science has known for a long time that skin colour is caused by the amount of melanin in the skin. That's a *description*. It's not saying that there should or should not be a lot or a little melanin in the skin. If it did, it would be *prescriptive*.

Our first big choice when we use grammar terms, then, is to decide whether to be descriptive or prescriptive. This gives rise to the question: what or who are these grammar terms for? If I want to learn a 'correct' form of a language (my own or another) then I might indeed want prescriptive grammar terms. Whether as a native speaker or a foreigner, I might want to know the difference between saying 'we was' and 'we were'. The answer is that 'we was' is a local or regional form, or it's a form belonging to a certain social class in a given region, and 'we were' is what is called the standard form – though it would be more accurate to call it the 'standardised form'. That's to say, the one that was agreed over several centuries to be 'standard' and 'right' when it comes to producing most kinds of formal writing. That's not to say that the standard is unchangeable. The standard form of writing and speaking has changed and goes on changing. One example: when I was at school, we were told that we must never use contractions like 'don't' and 'can't' when writing standard English. Now, in newspapers, books and formal writing, contractions are often 'allowed'.

A problem arises as to the status of the two forms – standard and non-standard. Is the standard form really the 'correct' form? Does saying it's correct suggest in some kind of secret or imperceptible way that a person who says 'we were' is a better person than someone who says 'we was'? There's no escaping that these biases creep in whenever we talk about the way people speak.

So if some people say 'we was' and others say 'we were', there are some contexts – as when we're talking to language learners – where there's an argument for saying that 'we were' is the standard, and some may also say that it is 'prestige' or 'correct'. But if we put a language-describing hat on, we might say 'we was' is one way in which some people speak English. In fact, we can, if we want to, alternate between hats.

When we're teaching language learners we can talk of the standard form and when we're trying to describe the many ways in which people actually speak English, we can have our descriptive hats on.

But let's just pause there and ask: what do these grammar terms add up to? Do they help us understand how language works? (You will have noticed that I'm not sure that they were much help with my STOP example.)

Another analogy now: how is a pile of bricks different from a wall? The wall is a structure where the bricks are stuck together in a pattern or several patterns. The grammar terms overall, as a whole, are an attempt to describe how and why the bricks (words) are stuck together to make a wall (speech or writing). But do these grammar terms do the whole job, most of the job or only some of the job?

As with the human body (anatomy and physiology), the grammar terms try to describe what's there and 'how what's there, works'. So far, so simple.

But why might any of this be defective?

For a start, we find from, say, textbooks in schools, that nearly all of these descriptions are focused on how we *write* and hardly any of it is on how we *speak* and *talk* to each other. In a way this is odd, isn't it? In our lives, we spend much more time speaking than we do writing. This matters because when we look very closely at how, say, people talk to each other, we find that it's very different from how we write a page like the one you're reading right now. How so?

In speech we hesitate, correct ourselves, repeat ourselves, tail off halfway through something, interrupt ourselves, use 'fillers' like 'y'know' and use a lot of words like 'it', 'he', 'she', 'they' (pronouns), whereas in writing we have to do more naming of these people or things to be clear who or what we mean. In conversations, we nudge each other along with words of agreement or disagreement and exclamations. We can also help each other by picking up on what someone has just said, by repeating or adding. The structure of what we say is likely to be different too. For example, when we write, many of us are more likely to use expressions that begin with words like 'because', 'although', 'while', 'whereas', 'if', 'even though', in comparison to when we're speaking. In addition, as with my example of 'we were' and 'we was', we find that people speak in thousands of other ways that are different from standard written prose. This is the huge, fascinating history of the use of local, regional, group and class accents and dialects. The conventional and prescriptive way of teaching grammar terms is to either ignore this or to diminish it by treating all this as deviant or defective.

Then again, within the matter of 'how we write', nearly all of the grammar terms focus on one particular part of how we write, that is, 'how we write sentences', while very little of it focuses on the systems we use to write longer passages or sequences of writing. What's more, within writing, nearly all of the teaching of these grammar terms is focused on one particular kind of writing – that is, what you're reading right now: what's called 'standard prose'. In fact, there are many varieties of kinds of writing and the usual grammar terms don't cover all of them. I list some later.

By virtue of focusing so heavily on what is a very narrow range of total language use, there is an implied suggestion that the way we write and speak is, or should be, governed by 'rules' and that these rules come from how we write standard prose sentences. I'm one of those people who doesn't think our overall language use is governed by rules. Conventions and patterns, yes. We can of course demand that in this or that particular piece of writing (e.g. a book review, a football programme, a newspaper editorial, a science textbook, an exam question), you must write in a certain way, but that's a rule for a particular kind of writing, not for language use as a whole.

If I approach the matter of varieties of speech and varieties of writing, with a view to describing each variety, I may well find that the grammar terms don't cover enough of what it is I'm looking at. Or, to put it another way, let's say I'm wanting to describe conversations; I may need grammar terms (or any terms) that include the conventions (rules, if you prefer) for, let's say, how we take turns when we chat to each other, or how we 'chain' ideas as we speak. If I'm looking at books with paragraphs and chapters, say, I may need terms to describe how a passage of writing – a paragraph, a chapter or a whole book – 'sticks together'. (In technical terminology, this is a matter of what are called 'coherence' and 'cohesion'.) These terms exist, but often appear as no more than an afterthought in the grammar books, as if grammar ends at the full stop at the end of a sentence. Speaking and writing are about much more than how we make a formal prose sentence.

Both in conversation and in some kinds of writing, many of the old 'rules' about sentences don't seem to apply – as we see in some ads, poems, song lyrics, play scripts and film scripts of naturalistic conversations, newspaper headlines, and in one of the most important ways we have of communicating with each other today: social media. Just think how much time we spend reading, writing and viewing (as with films and TV) these uses of language. Are they less important uses of language? Surely not. Are these uses 'wrong' or rather, can we say that they are various ways of being right? Are they less valid because they are not written in conventional sentences? I don't think so.

But there's another broader problem: as the linguist M.A.K. Halliday reminds us, the focus on thinking that our writing or speaking is governed by rules or by grammar terms overlooks the kinds of *choices* we make due to other reasons:

a) What we are writing about ('the topic or theme'). With every topic there are common or frequent ways of writing. Commentary to football (soccer) matches is very different from commentary to ice-dancing.

b) Who we are writing for ('audience'). As we write and speak, we inevitably try to make it suitable for a target audience – real or imagined. This guides us in how we write and speak: an infant schoolteacher talks to a class very differently from how a prime minister talks to MPs in the House of Commons.

c) The kind of writing we are doing (the 'genre'). If I am writing a song lyric for an audience of Country and Western lovers, or an ad for trainers (sports shoes), or a film script set in a working-class district of Baltimore for a film that I hope will be shown on TV, the language in each of these will turn out to be very different from what I would use if I were writing a science book about the history of the moon.

Each of these three factors contributes to why we speak and write in certain ways. Some linguists go further: we can't describe and explain how we speak and write unless we include these three factors: topic, audience and genre. As a tip for writing: every time you sit down to write, ask yourself about these. What's my topic? Who am I writing for? What kind of writing is this? You'll find it's a bit like giving yourself directions or a steer: 'head this way as you write'.

I don't suppose you came to this book or these pages for me to give you a grammar lesson (that is, a lesson in how we name and use grammar terms). It would be good if you hadn't been expecting that, if for no other reason than that there are plenty of grammar books already out there and even more online. I would recommend David Crystal's *Rediscover Grammar*, the online Cambridge Grammar, and Penguin's *Dictionary of English Grammar*.

'One from Wiltshire still in use today: "you've got more chance of chucking shit up on the moon" (impossible task).'

Ruth Behan

'From my mother and her family from Preston, Lancashire:

- "It looks like Paddy's market in here" (untidy)

- "If he were singing for ale he wouldn't get a gill" (terrible singer)

- "Weer's thee fotchings up?" (where/how were you brought up – someone who is being uncouth)

- "Fain to wick" (good to be alive)'

Sam Richards

Silly questions have silly answers, and here are some of my favourite responses to those whats, wheres and whys. I've heard so many brilliant versions from friends, listeners and followers:

'What's that? "It's a whim-wham for a goose's bridle."'

@paddyhughes59

'When I asked my gran "What's that?" as I often did, her reply would be: "It's a wip-wap for a wowser to wind the sun up." It may have been a northern saying, as I grew up in Manchester through the seventies and eighties.'

Julie Pollitt

'If you asked my dad the time, his reply was "Half past quarter to, met a bobby round the corner with a barrow full." Fortunately, I got my own watch for my eighth birthday.'

@theartcriminal

'My grandmother (a Yorkshirewoman) when asked awkward 'Why?' type questions and in a hurry, would reply, "Because there's milk in a plum."'

@CandiSpillard

'If someone was knocking and we asked who it might be, my nan would say, "Old Nick the bottle washer."'

@Aliveandmasking

'When I was a child in bed and heard someone on the stairs, I would ask, "Who's that?" and get the reply: "Icky with his eye out."'

Trish Bater

St Patrick's Day

St Patrick is the patron saint of Ireland, though if you were being pernickety (a nice word), you would say that technically Patrick was not formally canonised. With him being a missionary as early as the fifth century, he lived before canonisation officially came in. So 'tis said. However, St Patrick has been the Irish people's saint (along with St Brigid and St Columba) for hundreds of years, whether that be in Ireland or wherever Irish people have settled.

Some people from Ireland or with Irish family chipped in with some sayings.

'Here are a few hailing from family born in 1930s Cork: "too much taspy on him" (high spirits); "cat malogin" (awful, e.g. weather); "very correct" (a person with high standards); "that's gas" (funny); and one from 1970s Irish TV: "stop the lights!" – an expression of mock incredulity.'

@Carole_Lyons_

'My dad used to say, "We have the shakings of the hay dog" if we didn't have much to eat. He was Irish. I think dogs who ate hay would shake?'

Yvonne Dykes

'When we were getting ready to go out of an evening and dressed up to the nines, it was called "no goat's toe" in our house. My mother, from County Donegal in Ireland, inherited many odd sayings from her mother but this is one I still use.'

Bernie Holmes

In Northern Ireland and Scotland, the word 'slaters' is a name given to woodlice. In fact, woodlice have many different names in the English-speaking world:

- boat-builder (Newfoundland, Canada)

- butcher boy or butchy boy (Australia, mostly around Melbourne)

- carpenter or cafner (Newfoundland and Labrador, Canada)

- cheeselog (Reading, England)

- cheesy bobs (Guildford, England)

- cheesy bug (Gravesend, England)

- chiggy pig (Devon, England)

- chucky pig (Devon, Gloucestershire and Herefordshire, England)

- gramersow (Cornwall, England)

- mochyn coed ('tree pig'), pryf lludw ('ash bug'), granny grey (Wales)

- wood bug (British Columbia, Canada)

And there are more!

Quite why the humble woodlouse should be so rich in names is not clear.

More Irish expressions: thanks to Fiona Clark for all of these.

- 'Thick as champ' = not very bright.

- 'Face like a Lurgan spade' = a long face.

- 'Up to the oxters in clart' = up to the armpits in mud.

- 'Toby's hole' = hell.

- 'Banjaxed' = tired out.

- 'Arriving with one arm as long as the other' = bringing no contribution to a party or meal.

The Irish definition of a hypochondriac:

'Sure, he's always got an arse or an elbow.'

'My Irish granda, when he was tired in the evening, used to say: "I wish I had my stone licked and was in bed." This dates back to the Irish potato famine, when children were given stones dipped in a tiny amount of hot gruel as their evening meal. The gruel would dry on the stone and it took a while to lick it off, whereas that same meagre portion of gruel would have disappeared in an instant if taken on a spoon.'

Fiona Clark

Here is a wonderful selection of sayings from Amanda Preston:

My granny was born in Tipperary and raised her family in Glasgow. She spoke in a stream of rhythmic, often-repeated sayings and proverbs. Her sayings not only had a satisfying and comforting lilt to them, they also conveyed a life philosophy. These are just a few of her sayings that I remember and that guide my thoughts and actions to this day:

- 'The one that has the most sense has to use it' when two of us had fallen out and were being too stubborn to make up. It was a way of skipping over the focus on who started it and who was in the wrong.

- 'Ne'er an old sock but meets an old shoe' on unlikely but happy love matches.

- 'If it was a dog it would bite me' after looking for something that was under your nose all the time.

- 'Two heads are better than one – even sheep's heads.'

- 'There's nothing in my purse but tuppence and old holy medals' on the likelihood of getting mugged.

- 'Thank God we hae nane o thae worries' after watching one of her favourite detective stories whenever someone had been murdered for their money or for an inheritance. Always said with a good chuckle.

– 'Ye'll nae be so merry in the morning' when you were staying up late chatting or partying instead of going to bed.

– A common saying but so oft repeated by my granny that it became part of my way of thinking was 'Now walk a mile in their shoes' when you were being critical or judgemental, and in so many situations just: 'Be charitable, I say. Be charitable.'

How do we read?

Some questions about language seem too obvious to bother about. How about this? What does it mean 'to read'?

When I ask people this question, one of the first things that people go for is the idea of us deciphering, or what the jargon calls 'decoding'. Our letters are signs and we decode the signs. There. Sorted.

The only problem with that formula is that it doesn't tackle the matter of how we make the signs have meaning. I can make noises when I see a passage of writing in Polish, Hungarian or Icelandic, as they are mainly written with the same letters that I'm using for writing this book. But the noises I make have no meaning for me. This tells me that when I read, I not only decode, I find or make meaning. Or, if you prefer, I *understand* what's written, though I think saying that has problems.

So what does it mean to understand some writing? What processes are involved?

I've tackled this problem with my students at Goldsmiths University of London when they do a module called 'Children's Literature in Action' as part of an MA in Children's

Literature. They devise projects in which they try to find out how children think about books. Some of the researchers (my students) set up children talking to each other about a book, with a recording device listening to them, so that we then had the nice problem of interpreting what the children were saying. We started to devise categories for the things they said.

One problem with that: once you invent categories, there's always a tendency to think of them as watertight boxes separate from each other. In fact, as we discussed the transcripts of the recordings, we found that the categories we invented overlapped and merged. So before I put the categories in front of you, please bear in mind that the overall picture is much more fluid and overlapping than is represented by a list of categories. Imagine, instead, something much more squashy and porous (!) with one category influencing another or being used simultaneously with others.

That said, here are the categories that we have come up with. Apologies that the names of the categories are rather jargonistic. The explanation comes immediately afterwards.

1. Experiential-relational:

When we read, we relate aspects of our own lives (and/or the lives of people we know) to what we read. We relate what is in the text with something that has happened to us or to someone we know. One useful trigger question for this is simply to ask yourself or others: 'Is there anything I've just read which reminds me of something that has happened to me, or someone I know? Can I say why or how it reminds me?' This taps into how we feel about moments in any text without asking the direct question, 'What did you feel about that?'

2. *Intertextual-relational:*

This is where we relate what is in a book (or text) to another text. One useful trigger for this question is: 'Is there anything I've just read which reminds me of something I've read elsewhere, seen on TV, online, at the cinema, or a song, a play, a show? Why? How?' Again, this will help us understand how we feel about a moment simply by tapping into another moment from another text that we feel is similar – for any reason. It has been said that we read with what we have read. That's a simplification but gives us a steer, even so.

3. *Intratextual-relational:*

This is where we relate one part of the book or text to another part. One useful trigger for this question arises out of a moment in a piece of literature where we ask: 'But how do we know that?' And we answer that by using something that came before. (I have a nickname for this which younger children enjoy: I call it 'harvesting' – that is, collecting up information or feelings from other parts of the text.) We harvest all the time as we read. We harvest at the same time as we predict! And when we're predicting, that is an intra-textual activity as well.

4. *Interrogative:*

This is where we ask questions of a text, we voice puzzles and we are tentative about something. One trigger question for this is, 'Is there anything here we don't understand or are puzzled by?' This can be followed up by, 'Is there anyone here who thinks they can answer that?' And: 'Does anyone have any ideas about how we can go about finding an answer to that?'

In one sense a text is a set of puzzles, or we might say that the moment we start to read we are asking questions. One way to tap into this is to ask ourselves questions as a story or poem unfolds. Then, we might gather up these questions and see if or how we can answer them. This is a way of treating books as a process of investigation and we as readers play the game with the writer.

The writer might create situations that are inconclusive, mysterious, puzzling or intriguing and we ask the questions that the writer poses. Or we might come up with ones that the writer didn't even know they had posed. Or we might want to ask the writer a question (very likely). Or we might want to ask questions 'surrounding' a text, e.g. are there other texts like this one? What did people think at this time (the nineteenth century, say) about magic? Or was everyone a Christian in Tudor times? etc.

5. Semantic-significant:
This is where we have thoughts or make comments directly about what something in the text means. There are of course many traditional ways of asking questions about this. In an environment in which we are not 'telling' others what a text means and/or there is only one meaning, this can be speculative and provisional before anyone reaches conclusions.

6. Structural:
This is where we indicate we are thinking about or making a comment about how a part or whole of the piece has been put together or 'constructed'. These might be thoughts about, say, why a book is in chapters, or why something happens in 'threes' in a fairy story.

Hiding behind this question is the crucial one of 'form' or 'story syntax' or 'story grammar' and the like. That is, every time we read, we are reading something that follows or uses or plays with a literary form that already exists. They are like templates or blueprints. We have names for many of these: the detective novel, the rom-com, the sonnet and so on.

In terms of literary response, we will be more or less aware of these forms and these in part intermingle with our response processes. We do this through our expectations of how the 'grammar' or 'syntax' of the story or poem unfolds. Once we have read a few books which tell stories in a certain way, we start to guess what will happen, and indeed how it happens. Any book that is part of a series becomes more or less predictable.

One feature of children's and young people's reading is how they learn these structures, plotlines, motifs and forms, and build them into their responses. We can tap into these with the 'intertextual' question I mentioned above (in point number 2). The argument here is that reading one text is inseparable from the expectations we have based on our previous readings. They're based on what we understand to be the 'form' of other books.

7. Selective analogising:
This is where we make a special and knowing analogy or comparison between one part of a book and something from anywhere else (e.g. from our own experience, from another text, from something else inside the text). We think to ourselves that the moment in the book is 'like' a moment from somewhere else in our life or something else we've read or watched. When we do this analogising there will be an implied 'set' or 'series', as in maths, that we constructed around a motif or theme or feeling.

This process of analogising is extremely important even though it is often masked by seemingly trivial comments like, 'I remember a time when I was sad …'

The importance lies in the fact that we are involved in a process of creating an unstated abstraction. It is halfway (or more) towards abstract thought. Perhaps, it becomes fully abstract if we give that 'set' a name: e.g. 'sadness' or 'anger' or some such.

I believe that it is through this process of analogising that texts give us wisdom.

8. Speculative:

This is where we make speculations about what might happen, or what could have happened. This is any kind of thought or comment in the category of 'I wonder ...' or 'What if ...' We do this all the time as we read and we can collect these as we read.

9. Reflective:

This is where we make interpretative statements often headed by 'I think ...', i.e. it is more committed than 'speculative'. It's a considered reflection. They are more a response to the question we might ask of ourselves like, 'So what do we think of that moment/character/scene/landscape/cityscape etc?'

10. Narratological:

This is where we have thoughts or make comments about how a story or poem has been told, e.g. about narrators, methods of unfolding a story, what is held back, what is revealed (the mechanism known as 'reveal-conceal'), how we know what someone in the story or poem thinks, how we think or describe the fact that we go forwards and backwards in time in a story (this is a whole subject in itself: 'narratology'). It may include an awareness of how stories have episodes, or sudden 'turns' or 'red herrings', flashbacks, flash-forwards, etc.

11. Evaluative:

This is where we make value judgements (in our minds or in conversation with others) about aspects of a text as a whole. These can be comments about 'significance', 'what the author is getting at', or 'why someone in the text said x'. Or even, what the 'message' is, or 'what this is about', or 'what this story is trying to say'. They may well also be moral judgements about fair/unfair, good/bad, etc. Evaluative responses, in other words, can be those moments during a story or afterwards when we make value judgements.

12. Eureka moments:

This is where we announce that we have suddenly 'got it' – an experience that many of us have when we think we know 'who's done it' or 'why someone has done it'.

13. Effects:

This is where we sense that an effect has been created in us (or in others we have observed) because of the way something has been written. 'This made me sad.' 'This made me jump.' 'This made me laugh.' Keeping a response journal, or writing Post-it notes on poem-posters and the like, can 'grab' these very well. This can be a way of tracing what has been called the 'effect' – firstly by noticing how we are affected by a text (did it make me sad? happy? afraid? tense? full of hope? full of dread? why?) and also by looking to see what aspects of the text seemed to create the way in which we are affected.

14. Storying:

This is where we make a comment which is in essence another story. This is not trivial. As with analogising (above), it will almost certainly involve the making of a 'set' or a 'series', i.e. something has been selected from the original text in order to trigger off the new one. This is an implied generalisation or abstraction.

15. Descriptive:

This is where we recount aspects of the text. We might do this in our daydreaming as we read, after we have read, or in conversation with others later. This may well be more significant than it first appears, as we can ask ourselves why this moment was selected for the recount (i.e. 'Why have I described that bit of the story?'). Again, this may well be part of 'analogising' and/or 'storying'.

16. Grammatical:

This is where we find our attention drawn to the structure of sentences – the syntax, or how individual words are used grammatically. An author like Dickens varies his sentence structures enormously: one moment very long sentences with many clauses: the next, rapid-fire, short, sharp, repetitive structures. Why would that be?

One way to discover this is through reading or performing out loud.

If we ask of, for example, someone bossy in a text, 'How do we know he's bossy?' we may well find that the character uses a variety of ways to command people, not just the one. In other words, grammar makes 'sense' in many ways. It's the tools we use to convey meaning and we have many different tools to do similar things. So a character who is bossy might deliver orders like 'Do this!' or say, 'I want you all to …' Or, 'All children must …' They are all 'bossy' ways of talking, using different aspects of grammar.

We might find that the way into grammar is via different and differing 'clusters' of how characters show what it is they want, their motives and the like.

17. Prosodic:

This is where we notice or we draw attention to the sound of parts of the whole of a piece, i.e. the 'music' of it. One way to do this is to play my 'secret strings' game. This gets us finding links between parts of stories or poems, whether linked by sound or by meaning. These secret strings are the links between repeated sounds of letters, words, rhythms or the repeated or patterned way in which writers use images (similar or contrasted) ... or indeed any links we might find or make.

If we think it or say it and can prove it, it's a link!

Much of this is on the edge of our consciousness as we read because writers try to conceal it. Writers try to make links that are there, but affect us without words in the text saying that that is what they want to do. This is a crucial part of how literature is as much about feeling as it is about ideas. A key way in which writers create feeling is through repeated sounds, images and motifs. Some secret strings are between one part and another similar part. Some secret strings are because one part is in contrast to another.

These links are in fact different and differing kinds of 'cohesion'. Sometimes these are grammatical, as with first using someone's name and then using a pronoun ('Michael' and then 'he'), or they might be at the level of sound or image.

(Note in passing: you can argue that what defines literature is that it is a specialised form of cohesion!)

18. Effect of interactions:

This is where we notice or we draw attention to how people interact, i.e. how a person (any character) treats another, how they 'relate' and what is the outcome of how they relate. In my experience, this is more valuable than simply trying to describe 'character'. If we think of scenes or moments in literature, they end. We can think of these as 'outcomes'. A writer like Enid Blyton traditionally tells her readers what this outcome is: 'That served her right.' It is one of the marked differences between writing for young readers and older ones that these 'outcomes' are often more marked in books for younger readers. Even so, all texts leave 'gaps' in which these outcomes or effects of the outcomes are there for us to wonder about and speculate about. We dive in to these gaps and come to conclusions or mini conclusions.

19. Imaginative-reinterpretive:

This is where we move to another artistic medium (film, photography, drawing, painting, model-making, pottery, dance, music, drama, making PowerPoints, soundtracks, etc.) in order to interpret what we have been reading or viewing. This may well involve more generalising or abstract thought than first appears, because it involves us in selecting something from the original text and creating some kind of 'set' or 'series' with this, as and when we create something new. If pupils are asked 'why' this can be teased out.

(Passing note: this used to be thought of as one of the highest-status activities on the block. When we visit great mansions and stately homes, the ceilings and walls are often covered with paintings and murals of reinterpretations of classical literature. At some point in our idea of education we downgraded reinterpretation as some kind of artsy thing that is 'kinda nice for those who want to do it' rather than a profound way in which we can explore the ideas and feelings in a moment of a text or the whole text.)

20. Emotional flow:

These are the thoughts and comments which show how our feelings towards the protagonists change. Some people have invented 'flow maps' where you can draw up a kind of graph or chart, with the key moments in the plot along the bottom axis, and emotional states on the vertical axis … then you can label the line on the graph. This might be a graph, say, in which I felt more or less hostile to someone, or I was more or less amused by this or that chapter. You can create graphs where you have several lines, with each line representing a different emotion: fear, humour, tension, mystery. Then as the story proceeds, you make your line go up or down across the graph.

This is one of the key dynamics of a text. This is what writers spend hours trying to create. Writers are interested in trying to win a reader's sympathy for one character and the dislike of another. They may well want to play tricks by first winning our sympathy for a character and then 'disap-pointing' us by making that person behave badly. There are many variations to this flow that the reader experiences and it's necessary for the reader to make their own meanings, and come to conclusions and value judgements about whether things are right or wrong, fair or unfair, good or bad, nice or nasty, and so on.

But it's not just about 'character'. It's about the sensation of the moment or scene we are watching.

When we set up charts, we describe this emotional flow. And from these charts we can go back into the text to find why or how we think the writer helped to create this sensation. Or we might ask of ourselves, 'Why did I feel that annoyance with that character at that moment? What is it about me that thinks that kind of behaviour is arrogant?' etc.

Once again, there is an interaction between what we think is in the text and what it is about us that causes us to have that feeling?

We might ask of ourselves or discuss, 'Which was the most important "moment" when our emotions or feelings were flowing?'

21. 'Author intention':
This might come partly under the category of 'speculative' – see above – i.e. what the author could have written, might not have written, might have written in another way, or ultimately why we think the author wrote it this way.

Or it might be part of 'effect', i.e. how has the author created an effect. Word of warning: if this is separated from 'how it affected me' or 'how it affected someone else', this is of course speculation.

The routine of a good deal of 'criticism' is to assume precisely the opposite, i.e. if there is a certain literary feature – e.g. alliteration using a 'hard' sound – then it has a specific effect – e.g. it is insistent or heavy – and that the author intended this, which may or may not be the case. A huge amount of school-based criticism comes from this dubious premise: a specific literary feature has a specific effect. This can easily become formulaic and if it doesn't overlap in any way with your experience then it's just gobbledegook learned for exams.

We might encourage speculation about author intention by simply asking pupils, would you like to ask the author any questions? Then we might pretend to be that author, or ask someone else to do so, and we can interview them. Whenever we can't answer the question, we might ask ourselves how we can find out more in order to answer it. A book? The internet?

22. Contextual:
Every piece of literature comes from a time and place. The person reading or spectating it will not be in exactly the same

time and place as the author. Many responses and critical ideas and thoughts take place because of this gap. We may well know or speculate about the gap or the context ('They used not to do that sort of thing in those days') and, of course, we can go online and research it.

Between us we have very different awarenesses of contexts of a piece of writing. Give me an ancient Chinese text and I know very little. Give me a text written about London last year, I know a lot. Even so, for all of us there is always some context we know and some we think we know, and we bring this contextual knowledge to a text.

We can of course find out much more – and traditionally, texts by e.g. Shakespeare have a whole apparatus of 'context' around them that we are given in school. There are varying degrees to which this affects our response processes. Some of it may be so academic or distant that it has little effect. Some may be very directly affecting.

I have found in ideal situations the most affecting contextual knowledge comes from our first questions about a text or about an author. They are those puzzles and queries which hang in the air around a text.

We can draw these out, encourage the process of asking the questions and do what we can to set up the means of finding out. 'Is Roald Dahl still alive?' etc.

23. Representational or symbolic:
This is where we have thoughts or make comments about what we think something 'represents'. This might be about 'character', where we say that a person represents the class or type he or she comes from: 'She's a typical *x* kind of person'. It might be about parts of the landscape or the nature of the landscape, if it represents a particular kind of challenge to the protagonist. It could be a feature in the landscape/

cityscape, e.g. a particular kind of tree or building. It could be a single object that represents something more than itself – a torn piece of paper. And so on.

People often say to me that *We're Going on a Bear Hunt* is a 'bit like life' – you can't go over it, you can't go under it, you have to go through it. That's a representational thought and comment.

24. Extra-textual:

These are thoughts or comments that have apparently nothing to do with what's in the text and are about what's going on somewhere else, or they are about the interactions in the room at that very moment. Often these are as they seem to be but, just occasionally, they may well relate to how we are interpreting a book.

25: Causational:

These are the thoughts or moments when we say or think that something happened or someone thought something was because of *x*. In other words, this occurs anytime we say to ourselves, 'Oh, that's why she ...' These moments of realisation of cause (or imagined cause) are crucial to how and why we read. Part (a very important part) of the human mind hunts for explanations and reasons. We are drawn to wanting to know people's motives and the outcomes of those motives. This is at the heart of fiction and narratives of many kinds – perhaps of life too. We ask ourselves questions like 'Why did he do that?' all the time.

What other processes – stand-alone or overlapping with any of the above – would you put into this matrix of response?

Here's another of my own family phrases that has stuck. When we told my father that we were expecting a baby, he replied straightaway with, 'Planned or unplanned?' (Note: not 'Well done!' or 'That's nice!') We've made it a catchphrase for any event, disaster, mishap or surprise.

'My dad used to have two words for little children. A general term for toddlers and younger babies was "the widgers". If he met a child who was a bit older, he would invariably say, "Hello, Snodgrass!" Anyone else?'

@markswan52

'My aunt used to say of someone who was really nosey, "He/she would go up your arse to see if your hat was on straight." Makes me smile every time I think of it.'

@BridgeBooksDrol

'One that I only ever heard from my granny brought up around Yarmouth: "Smell the mange!" (pronounced as per "blancmange"). An exclamation when breathing in the briny fresh air at the seaside.'

@revlow

A real favourite from a follower:

'My father has started his own historical measurements system based on the life of Jane Austen. "That's 437 years before the birth of Jane Austen", "Jane Austen had only been dead for seven weeks when that happened", etc. It's quite difficult to follow.'

@Liberty_Rowley

Some things that our parents (or anyone in our family) say, become family legends and get repeated over and over again. This one was first a spontaneous outburst of frustration from my father but was recycled many times, anywhere, any time of day, when it seemed to fit the moment. My brother often reminds me of it.

'You come into the country for a bit of peace and quiet and all you can hear is mad Michael shouting his bloody head off.'

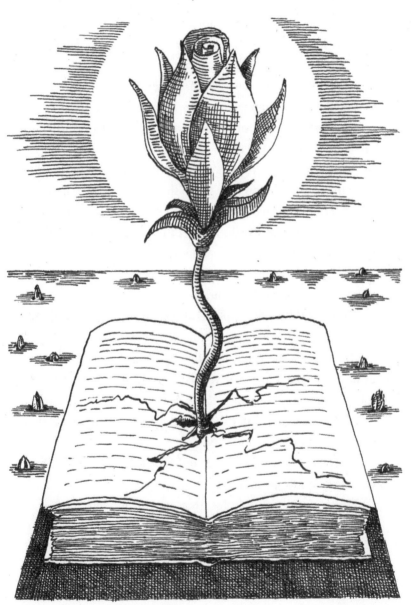

April would be as good a time as any to think about change. One of the most obvious and yet most contested facts to do with language is to say that language changes. In actual fact, languages don't change; we change them. This drives some people spare when they hear new words, expressions, pronunciations, changes in usages and much more. I can't think of the number of times people have pleaded with us on *Word of Mouth* for us to cover, say, why people seem to be saying 'so' when they start to speak; why 'young people' raise their voices when they get to the end of every sentence; why people say, 'I would of done it'; how broadcast journalists emphasise odd words, as in 'I'm standing outside THE palace right now, and IN a minute, I hope to be speaking to THE Prime Minister ...'; why management started talking about 'going forward' ... and so on.

No one I know of complains about why we don't say 'doth' or 'methinks' any more, as in 'the lady doth protest too much, methinks', but then that was first spoken in a performance in around 1600. In other words, we find it much easier to tolerate the fact that people have changed the language over hundreds of years, than the fact that we are changing the language right now.

In celebration of change and April, let's look at what Chaucer had to say about it.

Here's the opening to his great narrative poem (or is it a verse-novel?), *The Canterbury Tales*.

If you've never read Chaucerian English before, just let the words float through you, letting yourself guess or feel what they mean. A modern English verse translation comes next – note that it isn't a word-for-word literal translation:

Whan that Aprille with his shoures soote,
The droghte of March hath perced to the roote,
And bathed every veyne in swich licóur
Of which vertú engendred is the flour;
Whan Zephirus eek with his swete breeth
Inspired hath in every holt and heeth
The tendre croppes, and the yonge sonne
Hath in the Ram his halfe cours y-ronne,
And smale foweles maken melodye,
That slepen al the nyght with open ye,
So priketh hem Natúre in hir corages,
Thanne longen folk to goon on pilgrimages,
And palmeres for to seken straunge strondes,
To ferne halwes, kowthe in sondry londes;
And specially, from every shires ende
Of Engelond, to Caunterbury they wende,
The hooly blisful martir for to seke,
That hem hath holpen whan that they were seeke.

When April with his showers sweet with fruit
The drought of March has pierced unto the root
And bathed each vein with liquor that has power
To generate therein and sire the flower;
When Zephyr also has, with his sweet breath,
Quickened again, in every holt and heath,
The tender shoots and buds, and the young sun
Into the Ram one half his course has run,
And many little birds make melody
That sleep through all the night with open eye
(So Nature pricks them on to ramp and rage) –
Then do folk long to go on pilgrimage,
And palmers to go seeking out strange strands,

To distant shrines well known in sundry lands.

And specially from every shire's end

Of England they to Canterbury wend,

The holy blessed martyr there to seek

Who helped them when they lay so ill and weak.

[from Towson University's online translation]

We can see then that Chaucer wrote in English but not in the same way that any of us speak today. The word 'soote' means 'sweet', 'swich' means 'such' and when Chaucer wanted to say how folk 'long to go', he writes that they 'longen ... to goon'.

Why did people not want to go on talking and writing like that? No one really knows!

But here is April itself in Chaucer's eyes, also being a matter of change, quickening the shoots and buds and stirring people to want to go on pilgrimages.

As for why we call it April, it is by no means clear. The English name is taken from the Romans – 'Aprilis' – but it's not known for certain why they called it that. One suggestion is that it comes from the verb 'aperire', meaning 'to open', which also gives us the word 'aperture'. That works: buds open!

Before the moment when the people who spoke Old English switched to the Latin names for months, they called April 'Eostre-monath' or Easter-month, named after the goddess of spring, Eostre.

So this time, no change: we think of Easter as a Christian festival, but the name itself in English is pre-Christian. Long after people in Britain had converted to Christianity, they must have wanted to go on saying 'Easter' even though the language of Christianity in Britain talked of it as 'Pascha'.

There are many words for useless things and people. Here are some of my favourites:

'My mum's best sayings were about useless people and items. My favourite was: "about as much use as a chocolate teapot". Whenever I find myself looking for that analogy, it's perfect.'

@chris_swan

'My granny once described a fruitless endeavour in the following terms: "That's as much use as shoving boiled snow up your arse." I have no idea what that even means but it cracks me up.'

@tattooedselkie

One of my own. The army word for unnecessary paper-work was 'bumf' – supposedly from 'bum-fodder', meaning loo paper. In the Rosen household, we used that method of making a new word, for referring to various kinds of animal jobbie, by calling it 'dogsh', 'catsh', 'cowsh' and 'horsh'.

And one more. Another way of talking about being a bit gormless is when we say, 'Oh, I thought it was this way …' or some such.

The reply can be – as said by my best friend at school, who got it from a very aged grandmother, born in the 1870s – 'You know what Thought did? He piddled in his pants when he thought they weren't there.'

Or 'You know what Thought did? He followed a dung cart when he thought it was a wedding.'

And a third one from my own family. If my father saw anything useless or if we did something hapless, my father would say, 'Strictly from hunger.' I knew it was American, but I've just discovered that it was the name of a column in the *New Yorker* by S.J. Perelman, who worked with the Marx Brothers.

What are words?

In the beginning was the word …

… but was it?

Is that how language began? When zoologists listen to primates communicating, are they words? When we communicate to each other (or to ourselves!), do we do this in words?

There's a way of thinking about language as if it's made up of words, and at first glance it's obvious and true to say that. The sentence you've just read is laid out on a page, word by word, each with a gap between them. There is a slight problem with what grammarians call 'contractions' – the 'there's' and the 'it's'. Is 'it's' one word or two words collapsed into one? If a word is a single communicative unit, then 'it's' is a word. At the moment that I write it or say it, 'it's' does the job of a single word. But then, we might say it 'represents' two words, 'it is'. (By the way, interesting that when I say 'it is' I'm actually say 'it iz', but when I say 'it's', I pronounce it 'itss'. Another reason for saying that 'it's' is its own word, perhaps?)

There's another kind of problem with saying that 'language is words'. A pile of bricks isn't a wall. A pile of words isn't language. You can try this out in the safety of your own home. Take a dictionary and open random pages, shut your eyes, and put your finger on a word. Make a list of the words you find. Here's one I made earlier:

adjourn
carotid
devil
hand
open
stay
often
ladle
elf
arms

This doesn't fit any usual definitions of what language is because it doesn't 'stick together'; it's not coherent. Readers like yourselves can find meaning in each of the words, and you may even try to make it make sense! I'm busy trying to order a carotid devil-hand to adjourn, and then open up a ladle-elf's arms. By doing this, I'm trying to find some grammatical (syntactical) links. I'm trying to 'build a wall' with the word-bricks I found in the dictionary.

(It's also a great game to play. You can do what I've just done here, or play it in a group taking turns with just three or four words, and then see if you can make up a story using those words.)

There's another problem with focusing on words alone: I can turn myself into a Martian, and listen to some people chatting. I can make a note (in my head or in my Martian notepad) of the sounds I hear. I learned my English at a very straight orderly Martian school, so I learned 'vocabulary' where I matched an English word to a Martian word. I have dictionaries and glossaries. I use Google by putting in 'translate Martian to English' (and vice versa, as we say in Martian).

My problem is that I hear quite a few sounds that aren't in my glossaries or dictionaries. Are they unnecessary shash, meaningless noises? Or are they units of meaning? I play them back over and try to write them out (using so-called Roman letters): 'erm, 'huh' and 'hah', 'uh-uh', 'waaa', 'hey', different ways of saying 'yes' like 'yep', 'yeah', 'yisss', 'yo', 'yerps', 'yih' … and many, many more.

My Martian-self secretly films the people talking so I can match what they were saying with the expressions on their faces and gestures with their shoulders, hands and arms. I notice that English-speaking humans can use 'erm' aggressively, meaning something like, 'you're talking rubbish', or they can use it as a warning, as in, 'I think you're stretching the argument a bit there'. Or it can just be that they can't think what to say next. Or even that it can be like a rhythm thing, creating a beat to what's being said. Here's someone quite famous doing just that:

> You've got the mega-investments coming in from … uh … Nissan, contrary to what … uh … some people said, prophesied and you know the Envision … uh … gigafactory investment as well. You've got the economic investment coming in at … uh … Darlington …
>
> [Boris Johnson, *BBC Politics*, North, North East and Cumbria, 3 October 2021]

What happened here was that the naming of 'Nissan', 'some people', 'gigafactory' and 'Darlington' was given a kind of trigger or 'trip' with this 'uh' (which is actually more like an 'ah'). It was this speaker's particular way of underlining or emphasising things.

We can make 'oh' be a word of surprise, disappointment or pleasure just by how we say it and the facial expression that might go with it. 'Hey' can be 'you over there' or some kind of ironic word, as with 'but hey, what do I know?' 'Waaah' can be mock-horror, mock-surprise or a comic-book baby-crying noise; 'uh-uh' can be a genuine warning to a child not to touch or a mocking version of this for adults meaning, 'I didn't want to go there/do that/meet him'.

And there are a hundred ways of making 'mmm' and 'hmmm' mean things.

In fact, we each have a huge repertoire of these words, helping us express ourselves, communicate with others, help us say what kind of person we are, what kind of person we think other people are and so on.

Meanwhile, another huge repertoire of non-word words has grown up on social media: the abbreviations, acronyms, emojis, emoticons and the like. It really doesn't matter what any observer thinks of these other than to say that they have become how millions of people communicate with each other every day, all of the time. That in itself is remarkable. After all, no one had any lessons in how to do this. No one did a course in them in order to get better at it. There was teaching, in one sense of the word: we taught each other how to do it. We asked each other things like, what does ROTFLMAO mean? If we liked it, we used it. It spread. And it spread in a similar way to people repeating 'through a glass darkly' (the Bible), 'a rose by any other name' (Shakespeare) or 'it's not even the beginning of the end' (Churchill).

Let me finish with LOL. The earliest moment it's been spotted by the *Oxford English Dictionary* (*OED*) is 1989, on the online news site FIDO. It may well have been used for some time before that. It is of course an acronym for 'laughing out loud'. If I drop it into the dump of 'acronym' or 'exclamation' then I really won't be doing it justice. The point is we can make LOL do a lot of work. One of them is the common schadenfreude LOL or LOLS that I use regularly when texting my sons. We're Arsenal supporters. We take malicious and childish delight in Spurs losing. Thanks to LOLS, we don't have to say things like, 'Did you see that Spurs lost?' At full-time one of us might text the other with 'Spurs LOLS'. Or it might be a conversation: one of us texts 'Spurs' and the next texts 'LOLS'.

Job done.

If you're in any way grammatically minded, you might like to know that something else happened there. LOL was, we said, a representation of 'laughing out loud'. That in itself is a kind of contraction of 'I am laughing out loud'. It makes the 'I am' redundant. We do a lot of this. I say, 'You going out?' not 'Are you going out?' and 'You in later?' rather than 'Are you in later?' People say, 'Loving this', rather than 'I'm loving this'.

People made LOL a unit of itself that didn't grammatically fit 'laughing out loud', as with 'Great LOLS'. We turned LOL into a noun so we could magnify it. And of course LOLS isn't a representation of 'laughing out louds'! It 'pluralises' the acronym itself. Once again, we didn't learn this by doing a course. We invented a way of speaking and writing, and then we adapted it to fit our needs as part of our daily interchanges.

Just one tiny picture of how language develops and changes.

Liverpool is an extraordinary melting point of peoples, accents, dialects and languages. To name just some: North Wales, Lancashire, Cheshire and a host of peoples settling in a great maritime port – Irish, Scandinavian, Caribbean, Chinese, Jewish, those from different parts of the Indian sub-continent and so on. The jazz musician and singer George Melly was born in Toxteth, Liverpool, and told me once that the Liverpool accent was 'Welsh with adenoids'. He then demonstrated this by talking in a northern Welsh accent for a bit, before switching his voice through his nose. He claimed (and George claimed a lot of things) that the accent was caused by the fog coming in from the Atlantic up the River Mersey. Yes, George.

I was also told by the musician, composer and sax player Tim Whitehead (also born in Liverpool) that there was a campaign run by the Liverpool bus company that said this: 'Treat us fairly, travel early'.

This plays on the fact that some people in Liverpool city and surrounding areas would rhyme these as: 'Treat us fairly, travel airly', while others would say, 'Treat us furly, travel urly' (… if you get me).

In fact, there isn't one Liverpool accent. Across the whole Mersey area there are several, if not many. When the Beatles appeared on the world scene, people attuned to differences in accent could hear that the Fab Four had slightly different ways of pronouncing things. They also brought to the attention of the world several words that many of us non-Scousers had never heard before, such as 'gear', 'grotty', 'belter', 'wack', 'lah' and an abbreviation of their own (I think): 'fab'.

'My nan always referred to a role that required little exertion as "a Bobby's job". Not sure if it's a specifically Liverpool phrase, but I can't recall hearing it said by anyone else.'

@murphmanz

'My Cheshire grandfather used to say of me, the worrier of the family, "That lad'll meyther a nest o' rots." Translation: "That lad will mither (make anxious) a nest of rats." Still true to be fair.'

@regcrawford3

The former footballer and manager Ron Atkinson was born in Liverpool and is famous for great sayings, some deliberate and some perhaps not so much:

- On a goalkeeper: 'Apart from picking the ball out of the net, he hasn't had to make a save.'

- 'Well, Clive, it's all about the two Ms – movement and positioning.'

- 'I just wanted to give my players some technical advice. I told them the game had started.'

Another classic from Ron Atkinson:

'One of the reserves came up to me and said, "I'm finding it a bit hard, it's the first time I've ever been dropped." So I told him to do what Nick Faldo does and work at his game. Next thing I know he's doing exactly what Faldo does, he's taken up golf.'

More Scouse:

- 'Those sunnies are antwacky' (sunnies = sunglasses, antwacky = old-fashioned, unstylish).

- 'Got these boss new trabs and kecks off me ma for Christmas' (boss = very good; trabs = shoes/trainers; kecks = pants/trousers).

- 'Seen this proper divvy, like, selling jarg bifters' (divvy = stupid person; jarg = fake, not a real brand; bifters = cigarettes).

When I asked readers, followers and listeners for their favourite expressions, there were many about food and drink. Perhaps we're more interested in food than in the weather. Is that possible?

Tea is a special obsession.

'My grandmother would refer to weak tea as "water bewitched and tea begrudged".'

@JennyHesford

'My dad used to say to me and my sisters when we were children, "Now would you like a glass of Corporation Pop?" as though it were a rare and expensive treat. Corporation Pop is, as I soon discovered, tap water.'

@peterjrainford

Other replies in this vein mentioned 'duck wine', 'council juice' (Glasgow) and 'county council lemonade'.

'My mother came up with a phrase recently I'd never heard before when I gave her a cup of tea that wasn't full to the top – "That won't do, you're showing the parson's collar!"'

@spademashie

Another reader reported the same:

'Parson's collar, meaning when a tea or coffee cup isn't filled right to the top, such that a white circular band is apparent at the top (assuming the cup is white!).'

@OldratEssex

'"Fortnight tea" = "two week" to struggle out of the pot, for a particularly unsatisfying cup of tea (usually made by my grandad). From my grandparents in Stoke-on-Trent.'

@Chloro_Biphenyl

'"Drink up, I knew your father," when encouraging someone to finish their drink or have another one. No idea where it came from but we were from Southampton.'

@AngelaB83971802

What's in a name?

What's in a Name? is the title of a book by Sheela Banerjee (as well as being the famous thing that Juliet says in *Romeo and Juliet!*). The subtitle of the book is *Friendship, Identity and History in Modern Multicultural Britain*, which gives more than a hint of what it's about.

It's an account that's both simple and complex at the same time. Sheela uses the starting point that the names of our friends and family are on the tips of our tongue and in our heads all day long, but behind each of these names is a complex history of life, work, culture, migration and change. She begins with her own name. You may have noticed that Sheela is not spelled 'Sheila' or 'Shelagh'. You (like me) may have thought that Banerjee is an Indian name, which it is and isn't. The reasons for these two names are powerful signs or symbols of how Sheela's family have lived their lives, how the British occupied India, how Sheela's family dealt with how people viewed them. I won't tell her story but if you want to hear more about the book, you can find us on BBC Sounds chatting about it, on *Word of Mouth*.

In the book, we meet Marcella Gatsky, Liz Husain, Maria (father's name, Timotheou), Vicki Denise Marie Seneviratne and Hugh St Paul Whyte, along with many of their parents and forebears. It is, as I say, a complex picture: networks of life seen through the names we give each other. By the end of the book, we know much more about the kind of society we live in.

Reading the book also made me think that we can all play the same game. Simply by looking at the names of people in our families and the names of people in our life, what can we find out?

We are of course surrounded by names. Sheela focused on the names we are called, the names of people in our families and the names of friends, but every day, we talk of the names of houses, shops, cafés and streets; the trade names of all the products we use, from foods to clothes; place names; country names; the names of the institutions we go through, such as schools, colleges or hospitals; the names of the firms we work for ... on and on.

What would happen if we wrote for ourselves an autobiography of the names in our lives? It would be a mix of origins, rituals, culture, identity and feelings. It would demonstrate a key way in which the language we use is about who we are. A way that not only shows we inherit the language that people around us are speaking and writing, but also that we make language.

So let's play.

Why Michael?

I have no idea.

Not a good start.

My parents never told me how or why they came to call me Michael. There are no Michaels before me on either side in my family and I don't remember there being any significant Michaels among my parents' friends. There were some Michaelsons they talked about who were so poor I had to be careful that I didn't end up being like them. Mr Michaelson was so poor he was just a shlepper, my mum said.

'What's a shlepper?' I asked.

'The fella who shleps the stuff from the store to the market stall. Mr Michaelson didn't even own a stall, he was that poor. You don't want to end up being a shlepper.'

A shlepper?

Why would I end up being a shlepper? There were no market stalls in Pinner, in Harrow, in the London suburbs, let alone shleppers to shlep stuff to such stalls.

What was my mum on about?

Oh, it was just a way to get me to do my homework. Immigrant anxiety, I call it. The fear that one day I would end up not only being poor, but even poorer than they were when they were kids.

So surely not named after the Michaelsons.

Nothing there, then.

But nothings are significant too.

My parents wanted to forge a new life for themselves that was different in many ways from the lives that their parents and grandparents lived. If they had used one of the names from their families, I might have been Morris or Moritz, Frank or Fredman, Joe, Alf, Sydney, Lawrence, Wallis, Max,

Oscar or Jeschie, Martin or Chil Majer ... but I wasn't. (Those names with an 'or' between them each tell a story in themselves!)

If you know about the traditional way in which Jewish men are named, you might be asking yourself, 'What about Michael's Hebrew name?' That's because traditionally, a Jewish boy is given a Hebrew name at the time of his circumcision. Now I lived 77 years of my life knowing two things about myself: that I'm circumcised and that I don't have a Hebrew name. Easily explained, I always thought: my mum told me that a lot of boys were being circumcised at birth in hospitals and nursing homes in the 1940s and 50s, not just Jewish boys. I was one of them. 'Done' as we used to say, by a doctor. Being in the showers at secondary school confirmed she was right about some non-Jewish boys. We called ourselves 'Roundheads' or 'Cavaliers'. More names! On reflection, a strange way for the English Civil War to survive in the popular imagination. You can imagine that the first lessons we had on Oliver Cromwell and Charles I had us grinning at each other from behind our textbooks.

Then, one day, in a flurry of emails between my brother and me, he revealed to me that in fact I was 'done' at home. What?! How did he know? Because he was watching. What?! I had lived 77 years and no one had told me before – not my mother, father, aunts, uncles, grandparents or my dear brother – that a mohel came to our house and 'did' me?! (A mohel is a man trained to do circumcisions.)

So now for the next nothing: did I receive a Hebrew name at my circumcision? For 77 years I've assumed that I didn't. But now I think perhaps I did. Perhaps at the moment of the 'snip', in May 1946, a name was said. And then that name disappeared into the air of 30A Bridge Street, Pinner, Middlesex ...

But why didn't anyone ever tell me this story until 2024? And, given that my parents were devoutly not-devout – firmly secular, in fact – why did they invite a mohel into our flat to 'do' me?

Ah, and there lies another story. Would it have been my father's parents? No, my father never knew his father. My father was born in the US, his parents split, his mother brought him, his sister Sylvia and his brother Wallace to London and my father's father stayed from then on in the US. So that puts my father's father, Morris (originally Moritz), out of the picture. His mother, Rose, was secular too. (As a child I loved saying that my grandmother was called Rose Rosen and that she was known as Rosie Rosen. Some names are little poems, aren't they? In fact, my mother's nickname for my father was Rosie too. 'Hey, Rosie, don't walk so fast!')

Now to my mother's parents. I knew them by their Yiddish terms, Bubbe and Zeyde (Granny and Grand-dad). More names of a kind. They were more traditional and 'observant'. I have no way of knowing for certain as my parents have died, but the flurry of emails between my brother and me ended up with our conclusion that I was 'done' because Bubbe wanted it that way. But as for whether I've got a Hebrew name – I don't know. Will I ever find out? Is there, somewhere buried in my father's papers or perhaps in papers inherited from Bubbe, my Hebrew name? Or in the archives of the Pinner 'shul' (synagogue), is there the little fact that Michael Rosen was given the Hebrew name of …?

But why the secrecy? This speaks of mixed feelings, change, transition, even confusion perhaps. And it's not the only secret. Of course not! What is a family if it isn't the place where we keep secrets?

I have a secret brother – one who came between my older brother and me, and who died before I was born. As I've related in my book *Getting Better*, I only found this out because one day, my father, my brother and I were going through old photos. One photo was of my mother with a baby on her knee. I asked my father whether that was me or my brother and he revealed for the first time (I was about 11), that this was the baby who died. His name was Alan. Another name that isn't linked to anyone I know of.

From that time on, my father hardly ever spoke of him, or said his name. My mother, never. There were no pictures of him on a sideboard or in a glass cabinet. He was never mentioned when we all sat together at mealtimes or on long, long camping holidays. No uncles, aunts, grandparents or family friends ever mentioned him.

Another nothing.

From that time on, I didn't know if he was buried some-where or whether he had a stone in a cemetery. Then, sometime in 2023, in the midst of my many family-tree researches, I realised that I hadn't researched Alan. I had allowed the nothingness of Alan to keep him even more blank than he needed to be. After all, I had excavated the heart of Nazi records in country villages and towns in France to find out about the fate of my father's uncles and aunt, and yet I hadn't tapped into archives right here in London to uncover Alan Rosen.

So I did.

And that's why in 2023, I found:

Alan David Rosen
died 17.07.45
East Ham Cemetery

Section Q
Row 25
Plot 44

But was there a stone? Modernity has an answer to questions like this. After one simple enquiry, the guardians of East Ham Jewish Cemetery sent me back an email with a picture of Section Q, Row 25, Plot 44.

There was nothing there. It's an empty plot.

As you might expect, I have no idea why he was called Alan but the discovery in 2023 for the first time in my life that his middle name was David rang bells. My father's best friend at university was David. I knew David. He was an engaging, high-pitched, fast-talking, hand-waving medic of some kind – a job which, as a child, I didn't understand. Respectful whispers passed around that David had discovered something important to do with embryos.

By the time I came to look at that name Alan David Rosen in 2023, David was also the person who had featured in a story my father told, about the freezing Berlin winter of either 1946 or 1947. The story went that David's mother sent my father in his US Army uniform on a strange trip to the cellars of the Berlin Natural History Museum in the bombed-out city to deliver a food parcel to Herr Professor Dietrich. The museum had also been bombed and the skeleton of a giant *Diplodocus* (sibling of the one in the London Natural History Museum) stood in the snow.

That David.

But also the David who was a professor and lecturer at Middlesex Hospital when I began my soon-to-be aborted medical training, still talking fast, waving his hands about, explaining the science of how cells in an embryo differentiate themselves and become specialised. Like … how we become humans. Important stuff.

But also the David, who, when I arrived late to one of his lectures in the jacket that had appeared mysteriously one day from America in a parcel of 'effects' that had belonged to Morris Rosen (the father that my father had never known), while water was pouring from the ceiling of the lecture theatre, looked up and said, 'Oh, I thought you were the plumber.' From then on, proud as I was to wear a US plaid jacket like the one they wore in *On the Waterfront*, my fellow medical students couldn't resist calling me 'the plumber'. Another name.

That David.

And I haven't told you about my middle name. I may not know anything about Michael, but I do know about my middle name. I am one of the oldest, if not actually the oldest English-born Wayne.

Of course, I can't see your face as you read this, but I know that when I reveal this to people, they fall about laughing. English Waynes don't look and sound like me, they think. And they're right. So why am I Wayne?

Remember my father in Berlin in the US Army? His best buddy was Wayne.

Growing up, I was proud of being the only person I knew called Wayne. I loved saying my name out loud in school when we had to say our full names. I loved spelling it out because people wondered if it could be Wain like the Scots and Irish word meaning 'child' or even, perhaps, the wain of Constable's *The Hay Wain*, reproduced on the walls of classrooms, friends' homes and on greetings cards.

Then one day, when I was ten, Wayne arrived. He was big, with a big voice, big American glasses, a big beard, a big family, driving a big VW van. He seemed to be the kindest dad I had ever met. When he drove the big VW van, he let his son Richard switch the indicator to indicate right and left. No dad that I knew would let their son do that!

I was so glad I was a Wayne.

My father would sometimes say that he had received a big letter from Wayne and that it was about 'literature'. By then, I was doing literature at school, but the way Wayne talked about literature seemed very difficult. One of these letters was about 'the self-conscious narrator in *Tristram Shandy*'. What? What was a self-conscious narrator? And who was Tristram Shandy?

Then I did more literature. Then I stopped doing medicine and did yet more literature. Then a book came out that everyone talked about: *The Rhetoric of Fiction* by Wayne C. Booth. It was a big book. It was big on literature courses. It still is big on literature courses. Anybody who ever wants to write about the 'how' of the way novels are written often reads Wayne C. Booth, my dad's friend.

One day something awful and terrible happened. The Richard who was allowed to play with the indicator on the VW van was killed. His car broke down on the freeway. He opened it up to look at the engine, steam burst out, he staggered out onto the road and was hit by another vehicle.

Then another thing happened. My son Eddie died of meningitis. I talked to Wayne. He told me how the family had made a 'Dear Rich' book of letters that people had sent to them about Richard.

And then he told me that everyone will be good to me apart from one. There'll be one person who will say the wrong thing. I didn't know whether to ask him what was the wrong thing that this one person said to him. I waited. In the end,

Wayne said, 'Someone said to me, "At least, Wayne, you've got other children."'

I wondered about that. It was a bad thing to say. But then maybe, just maybe, was the person trying to say, clumsily as it was, that you can take comfort in loving your 'other' children? I do.

Wayne has gone too.

I once had the chance to interview him on the radio. Just as he was coming through London once, a book of the *Complete Poems of E.E. Cummings* came out. (How ee cummings would have hated that 'E.E. Cummings' way of writing his name – but that's another story!) I asked my producer if Wayne C. Booth, Professor of English at the University of Chicago, could review it. Yes, he could and did. I sat opposite my Wayne and we chatted ee cummings, one of the poets who had most influenced me when I started to write. And that's another story too!

Now I've got a bone to pick with that Sheela Banerjee.

When I started writing these words about names, I wanted to talk about how my father's grandfather arrived in Britain as Joseph Chaim Leib Chipyi but in London he was Joe Hyams; how my mother's father was born Fredman Isakofsky but ended up as Frank Freedman because, they thought, it would sound less Jewish (really?!); or how a friend's father was a Polish French Jewish guy called Nat Szynkman but really his name was Nuta Szynkman, known as Nath, and known by a French name when he was in the Resistance – and although he was arrested and put in Dachau Concentration Camp, they didn't ever find out he was Jewish because he had false papers with that French name.

Or how my great friend Malc had an Armenian name, an Armenian granny who made heavenly 'pilaff' and an

Armenian uncle who sat in a living room surrounded with old gramophones with His Master's Voice-type horns. Or how the doctor who treated me for a near-fatal illness was called Dr Gesundheit. Or how the Essoldo cinema chain was not named after a largely unknown Italian custom but after Esther, Solly and Dolly, Esther being the niece of my great-great-grandparents. Esther married Solly and they had a daughter Dolly. Essoldo! Or how those great-great-grandparents came to England called Bruchsztejn but became Brookstone and lived in Oystershell Row, Newcastle. Oystershell Row. What a name! 'Are we Geordies then?' my six-year-old son once asked me. But then I had lived in a road called Love Lane, I told him. Why was it called Love Lane? And why did my friends always giggle when I had to say in class for some reason, 'I live in Love Lane'?

Or how my children named our cat Smudge after Alan 'Smudger' Smith, our Arsenal hero, and once, when I was standing next to him for a wedding photo (not my wedding or his), I told the great Smudger that my children had named our cat after him. He seemed interested but not overwhelmed and added that though he had never heard of someone giving a cat his name, he had once heard of someone who had named a goldfish after him. Now there's a thought: a goldfish named after an Arsenal striker. Why not?

Or how was it there was a girl in our school with the Chinese surname 'Su'; or that one day in the middle of the north-west London suburbs in 1959, a boy arrived at that school called Sunil Das, whom we called 'Sha-neal', and how when he first came into the room, before the teacher told us his name, the Jewish girls were excited that a guy as handsome as that 'looked Jewish'... and wasn't all this, in a way, part of a story that comes just before Sheela Banerjee's stories, because she was brought up in north-west London too?

But there isn't room. Another day, perhaps.

But now you can play the name game.

Or this one:

Michael, Michael
Bo-bi-ichael
Bo-na-na
Fanna, fo-fi-ichael
Fee-fi-mo-mi-ichael
Michael

That's 'traditional' too and the singer Shirley Ellis, you may remember, did a great version of it: 'The Name Game'.

A particularly rich vein of phrases that came in was insults.

One phrase that seems to have survived – just about – from pre-decimal coinage, is calling people a 'daft a'peth', especially in the north of England. An 'a'peth' is a version of something that no one ever said: 'halfpennyworth'. But as with several of the old money terms, we used various versions such as 'tuppence' and 'thruppence', and there were and still are many slang terms for coins, like 'tanner' for sixpence, a 'bob' for a shilling and a 'joey' for a threepenny bit. And I knew people who called half a crown 'half a dollar' and loose change 'shrapnel'.

My own father used to describe a weak-looking sportsperson as 'all wind and piss'. One I liked from a listener is:

'They tossed up with a spuggy (sparrow) and lost', which was his father-in-law's description of someone with skinny legs

@jackofhearts74.

'If someone was a bit weedy physically, my granny/mum would say they "couldn't knock the stew off a bap". For years I thought they meant meat stew but stew is also a word for dust. So it meant they couldn't knock the flour off a floury roll.'

@KerryKe98646929

'I've seen more meat on a butcher's pencil.'

@MoyraMahoney

'"Sure, a bear wouldn't hug him" was a well-used phrase in our family. My nan handed this down to my young mam, sometime in the fifties … She came from Wexford and lived her adult life in Dublin.'

@mc_gwendy

'My mum would say, "She doesn't half fancy her barra" to describe someone boastful ("barra" means a barrow or a stall

from the market). She was from Edinburgh but lived in Glasgow at one point.'

@gortex2

'Quite a common Aussie one for shirkers: "They wouldn't work in an iron lung".'

@kevinmitchell50

And another from Kevin:

'From an old (Catholic) friend and gambler, who'd bemoan a timid wager: "They've a heart the size of a rosary bead".'

'My dad would say that a confused person "doesn't know whether it's highday, Friday or Sheffield Wednesday".'

@VelvetNoire19

'When I lived in Nottingham, I knew someone who used the phrase "a right greasy mildrew" to describe anyone who looked like they needed a wash and a shave.'

Lis Rosen Parsons

May

If we start with the first speakers of English in Britain, the Venerable Bede tells us that they called the fifth month of the year 'Three-milkings-month' (Þrimilcemōnaþ), where 'þ' is pronounced 'th'. You can see the ancestors of our words 'three' and 'month' in there. It was called this, says Bede, because there was such abundance in Britain and 'Germania' where the 'Angle-people' came from, that they would milk their cows three times a day.

This nice marking of daily life disappeared when people adopted the Latin name 'Maius'.

Scholarly opinion is divided on quite who is honoured in this name. One view opts for Maia from ancient Greece, who was daughter of Atlas, mother of Hermes (Mercury) by Zeus. Atlas, you'll remember, holds up the sky, so Maia was known to some as Mountain Maia of the beautiful black eyes.

The other view is that May is related to 'maiores' meaning the 'greater ones', that's to say older people who should take precedence – ancestors. (You'll see words like 'major' and 'mayor' in there too.) One of the Roman festivals held in May was a festival for the dead.

Either way, the Roman's treated May as a time of growth but also as an unfortunate month. On 1 May, the priests who dedicated their lives to Vulcan, the god of fire, sacrificed a pregnant pig in honour of Maia, a possible link to how the Ancient Greeks viewed her, as the mother who nursed Hermes and thus the goddess of nursing mothers.

The roots of May through Rome and ancient Greece twist around this mix of growth of the young, fire (warmth) and respect to ancestors. Some suggest a strong link to the idea of Mother Earth too.

It feels logical to many to link our 'May Day' to these ancient festivals and deities, especially the Floralia, a festival in honour not of Maia but of Flora the goddess of flowers. The Floralia opened with theatre shows. The poet Ovid tells us that hares and goats were released, crowds were pelted with beans and lupins, and games and sacrifices followed.

At other times, in the month of May, and with an echo of the name Maia, the Maiouma festival celebrated the union of Dionysius (god of wine and pleasure) and Aphrodite (goddess of love and beauty). By the time the early Christian father, John Chrysostom (approximately 347–407) got sight of it, he condemned what was going on as 'a sea of lasciviousness'. Some of the pre-Christian elements survive to this day as flower festivals and May Queen parades.

Then again, through a history of strikes and major disputes that took place in and around the beginning of May in the 1880s and 1890s in the USA, Australia and elsewhere, the international left-wing and labour movement adopted 1 May as a 'Labour Day' and a holiday. Thus: May Day.

Put together, this has all ended up as a lot of meaning and history packed into one very short word.

Another memory from the Rosen household. My father used to leave piles of books and papers around his armchair that he was 'working on'.

My mother would say, 'Look at your father. He's surrounded with his droppings.'

'My gran said you could always spot the professional women in a supermarket: "They're like the man with no arms" (whilst doing an impression of someone grabbing items willy-nilly, chucking them in the trolley regardless of cost). Shopping in a hurry is now an "armless shop".'

@jaxhampton

'After saying grace, my paternal grandfather would exclaim, "Piggly Wiggly!" which is a supermarket chain primarily in the rural American South. He was thanking the market for the food. Irreverent but accurate. He grew up in south-east Georgia in rural Bulloch County.'

@sevenpitches

'My dad (aged 91¾) has waved off three generations with a cheery "Toodle pip, see you on the ice, thank your mother for the rabbits." When asked why, he has no idea. "Something my dad always said."'

@flapdoodles59

A mysterious one from my own mother:

> Mum, entering my messy bedroom: 'This place is a mishadamonk.'
> Me: 'What's a mishadamonk?'
> Mum: 'This place.' (And then she leaves.)

'I had a friend who always said, "As long as there's a hole in the mattress, I'll see you in the spring!"'

@Mab_Taliesin

When two people meet up and start going on and on about their illnesses, ailments, aches and pains, a friend told me that they call this 'the organ recital'.

'My Irish granny would complain about a neighbour so mean that "she'd cut a currant in two".'

Ruth Hirschfield

The territory of the UK (technically the United Kingdom of Great Britain and Northern Ireland) and of Ireland has been an area that has seen both emigrants leaving and immigrants arriving for thousands of years. And it goes without saying that many of the emigrants come back. The effect of all this movement and mixing is that people who speak English in the UK and Ireland use words and expressions from the old 'root' languages such as those of the Celtic family, old Germanic languages (sometimes misnamed Anglo-Saxon), Norman French, Latin and hundreds of other languages from all over the world.

A Martian arriving in Britain right now would find that many people speak both English and other languages, particularly at home. Do you know which non-English language has the largest number of speakers in Britain? (I'll give you the answer at the bottom of this page.*)

When we mix languages we do it very freely, taking a word in one and making it work grammatically in another. To say you're very proud in Yiddish, you use the word 'kvell'. If you want to say you're proud now, you might say, 'I'm kvelling'. This is one example of thousands in how we're all very much at ease taking the word of a non-English language and putting an English ending on it (-ing) so that it works in English.

We not only 'borrow' words from speakers of other languages, we also translate expressions from other languages that follow the shape of the original, as with the phrase 'long time no see', which is the direct translation of a common Cantonese greeting ('Ho lui mo gin').

Over the next few days, I've included expressions from speakers of languages other than English:

'If you did something wrong and didn't own up to it, my Italian grandfather would say, "big lies have little legs."'

@ChristineCarr

'I say "gap-shap" meaning "chit-chat", inherited from my Punjabi parent.'

@smcardle45

I met an old friend in the street. His mother was of Indian origin living in South Africa. To mean 'all over the place' or

---

* The answer to the language question is Polish.

'all round the houses', she'd say, 'I've been rum tum tali.' He didn't know if it was Hindi or another language.

'The first time I said, "Saying 'pumpkin' won't make dinner," in front of someone not immediate family, they fell about laughing. I thought everyone knew it.

Turns out it's a direct translation from Tamil, my grandmother's first language. It means "deeds not words".'

@WrathQueenof

'My Jamaican grandmother says: "T'ief t'ief from t'ief, God laugh." (When a thief steals from a thief, God laughs.)'

@PatriciaCumper

'My great-grandmother was from Guyana and she would always say, "Well, look at story." "Story" was used whenever a situation involved drama.'

@DiggyDiaspora

'My inherited sayings are in Greek, which was my first language, but living in London I've passed them on to my children in translation. Some of my favourites, from my mother: "Those who have no brains have feet" (for when you forget something); "He put both her feet in one shoe"

(he made her life miserable); "Should I sniff my fingernails?" (how was I supposed to know?)'

Maria Margaronis

'Favourite sayings from my mother-in-law who was born in Montserrat in the Caribbean:

- "Well, my Auntie Betty" – a statement of shock and surprise.

- "Fighting the dull" – combating boredom.

- "What cat have a play with, dog want it!" – which means, some less well-off people turn their noses up at things that richer folk would value.'

Kate Simon

'In Dutch we have "op je qui-vive zijn" (to be on your qui vive, which also means to be alert or not to trust something/someone). A leading Dutch language site says it came to Dutch from the French "qui vive", but it originated in the Italian "Chi vi va?" meaning, "Who goes there?"'

@Grobbenbolletje

'Mum used to call goulash "goulpopo". It took me ages to realise she was trying to be "refined" and make a joke – "popo" being German slang for one's posterior, of course! She was from Silesia. (The last syllable of goulash, "-ash", can be pronounced "arsch" – i.e. arse – so that explains the jokey euphemism.)'

@L15per

'When I was little, my mum (originally from Worms) used to call me a "Babbisch Gütsje" when I had food around my mouth and on my hands. I just used the phrase and never questioned until I saw your tweet. I asked her tonight and apparently it means "sticky bonbon" in Worms dialect.'

@kidsstoryworld

'From my merchant seaman granda: sanfarian [from the French 'ça ne fait rien'] = doesn't matter. They used a lot of quasi-French on board, e.g. "no bon" for "no good".'

@Think_Reed_Line

'"San fairy anne" was how we heard it when my dad said it, as in, "Ah, it's all san fairy anne to me." He was wartime Royal Navy and from Liverpool. On reflection, it was maybe Chinese whispers for the French "ça ne fait rien".'

@Paula_D427

'I understand the equivalent of "This isn't the Blackpool Illuminations" from French dads is "Ce n'est pas Versailles." I wonder what attraction other languages use to describe an over-illuminated house to their kids.'

@Sharon2807

'A useful family word from my Belgian grandmother – spelling unknown as I never saw it written down – but it sounds like "flowsk" ("ow" as in cow), to mean having lost crispness as in biscuits etc., not quite the same as soft or stale. Always assumed it was Flemish but can't find it in any variant spelling.'

@paulineridley

'My whole childhood, my father referred to garlic as "knoblock". It took an internship in Germany to discover the derivation ("Knoblauch"). I still use the "English" form in honour of my father.'

@djansonsmith

'My grandmother lived in South Africa as a child. She used to say what sounded like "vokumbiki", meaning wait a minute. I think this is Afrikaans. It came back to me when my children were little; one of them uses it now she is an adult.'

@annao_tree

'From my South African side of the family: "You've landed with your bum in the butter", which you say to someone who's done well for themselves or got lucky (why that would be a good thing, I don't know!). I think it has Dutch origins.'

Jess Anderson

What's in a name? – a postscript

… And I didn't even get on to Rosen.

Picture a scene: I am studying German at school. Hot stuffy classroom, 20 or so teenagers in a grey school uniform. Teacher in her fifties, glasses, inclined to um and er quite a lot and break into giggles at surprising moments. One girl in the class even provokes the teacher to giggle by bursting out with a chain of giggling herself. It can delay the lesson for several minutes.

The teacher is teaching us Brahms's' lullaby. She has a good, high-pitched, piping voice. Off she goes:

Guten Abend, gut' Nacht
Mit Rosen bedacht …
[literally: good evening, good night, with roses bedecked]

When the teacher gets to this point in her singing, she gets going with a good bout of giggling. She points at me: 'Mit Rosen bedacht …' and giggles even more.

I look at her. I nod and smile. Best not to comment. But then I think there's something a bit odd about this. Fifteen years earlier she and my father (also named Rosen!) were colleagues. She taught my brother for three years. His name is also Rosen. Brahms's lullaby is hardly a rare song. It's a beautiful and popular lullaby. She must have noticed before that the lullaby contains our name and indeed she must have spotted it the many other times she said 'Die Rosen' (the roses) with one or other of us. Why is she giggling now?

Well, names do spark all sorts of reactions: giggles, smirks, shock, sneers and much more. The linguist Susie Dent has amassed a vast collection of 'nominative determinist' examples – Mr Carpenter who fits shelves, Mr De Ath the funeral director. I've sent her my Dr Gesundheit (which literally means 'good health'), the doc who took sight of my blood test and said to me in his deep American voice, 'Technically you're dead.' (Only a Gesundheit could say that with real authenticity.) I can never hear the word 'torpor' without transferring it to his American accent as he was so sure I should have been in one. Torrr-porrr.

So Rosen is roses. Why am I walking around with the name Roses? The first reason is that my patrilineal line takes me to somewhere in German-speaking central or eastern Europe. The Rosen names (Rosenthal, Rosenblatt, Rosengarten, Rosenbaum and the like) are common German names. Rather pretty – valley of the roses, rose leaves, rose garden, rose tree. It seems that one reason why German speakers adopted Rose names was as a trade name for working in the rose-water industry – a much-used perfume in medieval times. Surnames for ordinary people started to become necessary in medieval Europe as people moved from small village communities into towns. Put crudely, if there were a good few Jacks, it was handy to be able to distinguish between Jack the Butcher, Jack the Baker, Jack the Chandler, Jack the Faulkner (Falconer) and so on. Hans Rosenblatt could have been Hans, the guy who made rose-water.

Of course, there were many other ways of making surnames, for example by using place names, such as Bentley, Ramsdale etc., or appearance, such as Brown (hair), Little and so on.

The twist here, though, is that as far as we can figure out, the Rosens in my line are all Jewish. One possible reason for Rosen as a Jewish family name comes from the time when people were often known by their house-name. Throughout medieval Europe, houses in towns could be distinguished from each other by a sign outside their house. (Remember, most people were illiterate.) The great expert on Jewish names, Benzion C. Kaganoff, claims that for various reasons Jews became very attached to their house-sign names and often took that name with them, even though they had left the Wolf house, or the Loeb house (lion), Taube (dove), Apfel (apple), Birnbaum (pear tree), Gruenbaum (green tree). Clearly the Rosen-type names could fit in here too.

There's another possible reason though.

Kaganoff writes that, in the late eighteenth century:

> Emperor Joseph II promulgated an edict ordering the Jews of Galicia and Bucovina to assume permanent family names. Similar edicts were passed in Frankfort in 1807 and in Baden in 1809. And Napoleon's proclamations of Jewish emancipation in France, Hesse and Westphalia in 1808 were accompanied by laws requiring the adoption of permanent family names. Prussia followed suit in 1812, Bavaria in 1813, and Saxony in 1834. In 1845 the Jews of the Russian empire were likewise compelled to take fixed family names.

And there's one more twist. This scheme became a way of raising revenue. Jews had to buy their names. For those who couldn't afford to buy their name, then in some circumstances Jews were given mocking or insulting names, like 'Eselkopf' (donkey's head).

Kaganoff also hints that the reason why some Jews felt drawn to Rosen names was because it was a way of keeping a link to what had been a traditional patronymic and matronymic 'ben' ('son of …'), so ben Rosa meant son of Rosa. Just to complicate that, though, Rosa is not a Yiddish or Hebrew name, so if Kaganoff is right, this would be a cultural memory of a Sephardic Rosa (Spanish-Jewish in origin).

Many winding and inconclusive roads, then. But that's where the interest lies.

Alternatively, you can go down the route taken by the comedian Dave Gorman, which is to travel round the world looking for Dave Gormans. He met many Dave Gormans. Simpler is to sit at your computer and find them there. As I was writing this very page, I received an email saying, 'Are you the Michael Rosen who wrote "Induced Pluripotent Stem Cell–Derived Cardiomyocytes"?'

I'm not. Nor am I the Michael Rosen who is (or was) the world-renowned anaesthetist, or the percussionist, or the sax player. Nor am I the sex photographer, the world expert on German philosophy, the Milwaukee trade union activist or the former president of Tree Canada; nor the children's poet from Oklahoma who is in charge of the James Thurber archive. I met him once. We signed each other's books.

It's odd that we think of names as being so personal, so wrapped up in who we are, and yet you can come face to face with someone who has spent decades being called the same thing. There's a hint of doppelgänger about it.

Now that would be a good name to have: Michael Doppelgänger.

To end the month, here are some miscellaneous sayings that I've enjoyed hearing from you:

'My grandparents had an extra dustbin in the sixties and seventies which they called the "gissy swill" – leftovers for pigs.'

@AxionCustom

'My dad always said, "Let the dog see the rabbit," when something was broken and he wanted to see if he could fix it. I've since found it's a greyhound term, though he had nothing to do with that world. It always tickled him.'

@SiobhanA1969

'"Shilling a bucket of slop" – displays of affection deemed performative, from a Yorkshire granny, obviously.'

@AJellyfish

'If you see someone with trousers too short, you say to them: "Put jam on your shoes and invite your trousers for tea." One of my mother's sayings from the Isle of Wight.'

Brenda

'A "flo-dear", when you've spilled/dropped something. After the habit of a relation, Floretta, always dropping food down her front (she had an ample bosom, apparently). Her husband would say, "Oh, Flo dear."'

@JennyMLloyd

'My mum from Tyrone used to say, "Let the hare sit" – for situations best left alone – to see how they pan out. I still use it.'

Joe Duggan

Finally, one of my own to end the month. I was watching an old film with Ginger Rogers in it, and someone said to her, 'Honey, you're still in your robe.' I use it whenever anyone is in their dressing gown (including myself) after about nine in the morning – has to be said in an American accent.

The immediate source for June is the Roman word for June which was 'Junius'. So far, so simple. For anyone even only faintly knowledgeable about Roman gods and goddesses, there would seem to be an obvious link between June and Juno, the goddess of marriage and wife of the supreme deity Jupiter (also known as Jove). We might then guess that Romans would have spent many happy June days getting married and frolicking about in celebration of coupling.

Not so fast.

Even Ovid, the great Roman poet and etymologist, wasn't sure about this. Just as he wavered over whether the month of May commemorated Maia or the 'maiores' (the great ones), when it came to June, he was unsure as to whether it was in honour of Juno or the 'iuniores', the younger ones. This last, if true, would neatly match May's 'maiores' who came before. Perhaps. We have to live with uncertainty here.

The Romans loved to honour their greats with festivals and the like, and one candidate here would be Lucius Junius Brutus. He is not to be confused with the Brutus we know from Caesar's assassination. Lucius Junius Brutus was a founder of the Roman Republic in the sixth century BC. In fact, it's fun to speculate that Shakespeare might have wondered whether the life of this Brutus would have made an excellent addition to his portfolio of Roman plays, as he led a successful revolt against the last King of the Romans and went on to fight off several attempts by the royal family to stage a comeback. The idea of Shakespeare pondering over whether this would have made a good show is not as fanciful as it sounds, because Lucius Junius Brutus has a leading part to play in Shakespeare's long poem *The Rape of Lucrece*.

On the other hand, we have a hint from one great Roman writer that it was Juno and not Junius who was celebrated with the name: Plutarch suggested that June was a good month for weddings.

But without any certainty, we are in the strange position of having a key name in our calendar – and indeed in our lives – without any clear idea as to who we are commemorating or why.

The speakers of Old English had no such problem. This month was known to them as Aerra Liða-monaþ (where ð was pronounced like the 'th' in 'other' and the 'þ' was pronounced like the 'th' in 'thin'). The phrase means 'first sailing-month' or 'first travelling-month'. Once again, a very down-to-earth way of naming a month. Most parents of British school-age children gnash their teeth every year as 'flaming June' flames by, with only a few days half-term for a holiday. Then, when the big summer school break comes, it's quite common for at least half the holiday to be rained off. Clearly the ancient English folks didn't have to wait for the school hollies.

As we've done insults, how about compliments?

'"She's all there with her lemon drops" – one from my ma-in-law this time, used to refer to someone who is sharp, bright, clever and doesn't miss a trick.'

@KarenRedfern2

Even southerners like me know the word 'bonny' from Scotland. When I was 12, I even went so far as to stand in front of about a hundred French children on a summer camp in Normandy and sang 'My Bonnie Lies Over the Ocean' with the result that for the rest of the holiday the other French children sang it back at me as if it was my own personal anthem.

Not so well known outside of Scotland is that 'tidy' can be very complimentary too.

It's usually good to be called 'braw' by someone in or from Scotland. You'd be good and handsome, though it's a variant of 'brave'.

In the Midlands, if you say 'oil tot', it means you're satisfied and happy, as in: 'I'm in my oil tot.' It dates from the days when working men would have a tot of olive oil before drinking beer, in the belief that it would line their stomachs and stop them getting very drunk. Handy for saying something nice after you've been given some good food or drink.

At the end of a big meal my father put on a posh voice and sang:

> May God be praised
> My belly's been raised
> Half a mile above the table.

In the Appalachian Mountains region song sometimes known as 'Come All Ye Fair and Tender Ladies' but also as 'Little Sparrow', there's a double-edged compliment:

Do you remember our days of courting
When your head lay upon my breast
You could make me believe with the falling of your arm
That the sun rose in the West.

(It's double-edged because the song is about the fickleness of a lover.)

Slang terms to describe people appear and disappear very quickly. One compliment that's survived several decades is 'boffo'. It's been around since at least the 1940s, starting out in the US in the world of advertising, film, theatre and TV. It's not to be confused with a shorter version of the word that means something else altogether.

Altered states

You can call yourself anything you want. When I changed school at the age of 16, I restyled myself as M. Wayne Rosen. For some reason it infuriated my parents but I'm rather sad that I gave it up at 19.

So how about a quiz? No cheating. Here's a list of birth names of famous figures. What names are they famous as? See how many you (or your companions) can get.

In the spirit of the apparent idea that pseudonyms keep your real identity secret, but in reverse (if you get me), I'm not providing the answers.

It's interesting to pause a moment and think about what advantage they gained by taking on the pseudonym. Why did they do it the first place?

Stuart Goddard

Henry McCarty

Michelangelo Merisi

Ilich Ramirez-Sànchez

Giovanni Antonio Canal

Adolphe Mouron

Andreas van Kuijk

Dominikos Theotokópulos

Florence Graham

Josephine Mentzer

Giovanni di Pietro di Bernadine

Nguyen Sinh Cung

Choo Yeang Keat

Ioseb Dzhugashvili

Charles-Édouard Jeanneret

Emmanuel Radnitzky

Margaretha MacLeod

Agnes Bojaxhiu

Edson Arantes do Nascimento

François-Marie Arouet

Gloria Jean Watkins

Daniel Foe

Mary Ann Evans

Wilhelm Albert Włodzimierz Apolinary Kostrowicki

Georges Remi

James Alfred Wight

David John Moore Cornwell

Daniel Handler

Charles Lutwidge Dodgson

Samuel Langhorne Clemens

Marguerite Annie Johnson

Jean-Baptiste Poquelin

Helen Goff
Ricardo Eliécer Neftalí Reyes Basoalto
Allan Stewart Konigsberg
Nicole Françoise Florence Dreyfus
Alphonso Joseph D'Abruzzo
Timothy Alan Dick
Frederick Austerlitz
Lionel Begleiter
Don Glen Vliet
Priscilla White
Alison Clarkson
David Jones
Damon Gough
Richard Walter Jenkins Jr.
Nicolas Kim Coppola
Maurice Joseph Micklewhite
Barry and Paul Elliott
David Kotkin
Bernard Schwartz
Peter Moffett
Robert Nankeville
Doris Kappelhoff
Pauline Matthews
Elizabeth Grant
Calvin Broadus Jr.
Issur Danielovitch
Robert Zimmerman
Stefani Joanne Angelina Germanotta
Frances Gumm
George O'Dowd
Richard Grant Esterhuysen
Natalie Renée McIntyre

Audrey Ruston
Eleanora Fagan
Tracy Lauren Marrow
Gordon Matthew Thomas Sumner
William Michael Albert Broad
Reginald Kenneth Dwight
Krishna Bhanji
Arthur Stanley Jefferson
Lee Gordon McKillop
Peter Gene Hernandez
Farrokh Bulsara
John Eric Bartholomew
Édith Gassion
James Osterberg Jr.
Natalie Hershlag
Richard Penniman
Dylan Kwabena Mills
Ramón Antonio Gerardo Estévez
Eunice Waymon
Marco Salussolia
Michael Pennington

'My grandma says a well-to-do person is "very oomph-a-doodla".'

@VelvetNoire19

If my mum bent down on the other side of the room, back-side facing us, my father would say, 'Nice expression on your mother's face today.' In a similar vein:

'An old colleague of mine would announce such a situation by shouting, "Full moon over Burma!"'

@owenjell

'Over in Ireland they say, "Do you think I came up the Lagan in a bubble?" I've actually heard Adrian Dunbar say it on *Line of Duty* too.'

@sheenz_m_

'The London version: "I didn't just come up the Thames on a bike."'

@GregorRitchie7

'Another: "I didn't come down in the last shower!"'

@realjohncarvill

'Are you coming out ta lake?' Meaning 'coming out to play', from South Yorkshire.

[Several sources]

'"Quick the hurry" – from a fire notice in a Norwegian hotel seen by my maternal grandfather in the 1920s/30s: "To quicken the hurry, pull the plaited snotter."'

@JennyMLloyd

I watch a YouTube video series called *Yiddish Word of the Day*. In one episode, the presenter, Rukhl Schaechter, talks about the words 'kats' (cat) and 'koter' (tom cat). Rukhl says, 'Zi hert im vi dem koter' (she hears him like a tom cat) – in other words, not at all. I imagine ancestors chewing at each other … one of them repeats something he's just said. His wife says, 'I heard you the first time.' He mutters under his breath, 'Vi dem koter.'

'Do you want to know a Yiddish proverb?' our teacher says. 'Men ken nisht tantsn af tsvey khasenes mit eyn tukhes.'

It means, 'You can't dance at two weddings with one bum.' You can't do two things at the same time.

Eponyms

I was in Australia in 1987 and thought at first that everything that people were saying was obvious and clear. However, every now and then a word or expression would pop out that would have me floored. One of these was 'furphy'. When Australians say it, it's got a very distinctive flavour because the 'y' sound on the end of words in Australian English is a precise 'ee' as I might say the first part of 'eat'. So what is this 'furphy'?

It means a rumour or a bit of gossip.

But where does it come from?

At the time, the story was that it came from the name of the company who made the mobile water tanks that were taken to places in the outback. It was said that people gathered round them, swapped stories, and told 'furphies'.

But some people weren't happy with that explanation. Furphy also made the tanks to collect up the sewage from latrines, especially in the army. It was said, then, that when men sat in rows in their latrines, they told each other furphies.

Same company. Different kind of tank.

Either way, this tells us several things at the same time. With many words and phrases, it's very hard to pin down the exact moment someone or some people invented the word or expression. There are hundreds of books and online sites full of ingenious, plausible, far-fetched, obvious, obscure and erudite explanations for 'by the skin of your teeth', 'rule of thumb', 'boycott', 'in the slush pile', 'double Dutch', 'the plimsoll line', 'put your back up', 'you get on my wick', 'faster than you can say Jack Robinson', 'not over till the fat lady sings', 'push the envelope', 'blue sky thinking', 'elephant in the room', 'can of worms', 'Bob's your uncle', 'Davy Jones' locker', 'the real McCoy', 'the full Monty'... and so on and so on.

'Furphy' fits one particular kind of thing we can do with language: take a name of a person, place or thing and recycle it to mean something else, also known as an eponym.

The most obvious way of doing this is to take the name and add something onto it so that it can mean 'like' that person or place: 'Kafkaesque' and 'Pinteresque' are two literary ones. The writer (Franz Kafka or Harold Pinter, here) is seen to have created something distinctive or original that is then recognised elsewhere as a motif, or 'trope'. These can take on a life of their own if people use them without having necessarily read the originals. Any prolonged labyrinthine clash with authority, bureaucracy or the justice system, we can say is Kafkaesque, analogous in particular to what happens to Joseph K. in Kafka's *The Trial*. Long pauses and conversations full of non-sequiturs can be described as Pinteresque, analogous to scenes from plays like *The Birthday Party* or *The Homecoming*. We do the same sort of thing with 'Churchillian'. Any politician whose supporters or enemies claim is responsible for some kind of trend, policy, form of governance or economic system might find their name suffixed with a syllable or two: Reaganomics, Thatcherite, Bennite, Leninism. Some are hidden. It took me years to realise that when philosophers use the word 'Cartesian', they're saying 'like Descartes'.

When I was growing up, I didn't ever hear anyone say 'vacuum cleaner' or 'vacuum flask'. They were a 'Hoover' and a 'Thermos'. What a time to own those companies! Every conversation about cleaning carpets or keeping drinks cool was an ad!

If you're a scientist, you may if you're lucky get your name attached to a disease, a substance, a part of the body, a species, or any part of or process in the material world you have identified or examined. I have a chronic condition known as Hashimoto's disease. I was once 'doing a practical' when Krebs of the Krebs cycle walked past. I've done experiments to reveal Young's modulus and Boyle's law. My brother has a coral named after him. If you try hard enough you can get your name attached to an asteroid.

However, I didn't ever know that 'diesel' is named after Rudolph Diesel, nicotine after Jean Nicot and 'plimsolls' (also 'plimsoles' and, at school, 'plimmies') were named after Samuel Plimsoll MP.

These are the eponyms I find most interesting: the ones we hardly know are eponyms. I've discovered in that nerdy way we do when we're chatting with people and say, 'Do you know that …?' that not everyone knows that 'boycott' is an eponym, named after one Captain Boycott. I assure you I haven't made that up. In the 1880s, Captain Charles Boycott was an agent of an absentee landlord in Ireland. Nationalist leader Charles Stewart Parnell suggested that people should boycott Boycott (not that he called it that at the time). The word 'boycott', then, doesn't just have an etymology but a whole archaeological treasure lying beneath the surface.

It's said that 'sideburns' (those hairy bits men can grow down alongside their ears) are named after Ambrose Burnside, a general in the American Civil War; leotards after Jules Léotard, a lawyer who ran away to the circus; and the saxophone after Antoine Joseph 'Adolphe' Sax. Not that Monsieur Sax made any money from his great invention. He was Belgian and died in poverty in Paris.

You can also make up false pseudonyms and see how many people you can con with them: the Post-It was named of course by the famous Rodney Post, a man who tired of sticking notes to the wall with Sellotape and then having to clean the marks off afterwards; the mobile phone was invented in Mobile, Alabama; Roquefort cheese was named after an immensely strong rock-like man (Le Roque Fort) in Napoleon's army whose socks were used to create a bacillus which fermented sheep's cheese; to boris means to go on and on saying that you didn't deceive or mean to deceive even after it's been proven that you did, as in, 'Point of information – the previous speaker is borissing. I have evidence that he hid crucial evidence in order to misinform us.'

Over to you.

Here are some sayings in memory of my dad, Harold Rosen. When the conductor on the London buses used to call out the stops where the bus was going (in the 1930s), my father and his mates used to shout, 'Bang yer balls on the elephant's arseole, turn'em green and peck'em ripe' (Bank, St Pauls, Elephant and Castle, Turnham Green and Peckham Rye).

Sometimes my father was short of change and raided my money box.

> Me: 'When will you pay me back?'
> Him: 'Don't worry about that. I'd sooner owe it to you all my life.'

From a reader, also on the subject of dads owing money.

'My dad to me if I complained about something like that: "What's yours is mine, and what's mine is me own."'

@PeterJ2611

Here are yet more ways to describe the feckless, starting with a favourite from a reader:

'"Mauchtless" – although I don't tend to pronounce the "t". While the dictionary definition is "helpless, without power", it's used to describe someone a bit awkward doing something. Like giving someone a simple job and they try their hardest but just don't get it.'

@Cheese1138

Another from Harold Rosen. One of my dad's favourites about someone who was ignorant or daft: 'He doesn't know his arse from his elbow.' (I think that one's fairly well known, isn't it?) He would also sometimes say, 'His mind's as broad as a peanut.'

'My late mother-in-law didn't have time for unhelpful or unpleasant people. She would always say: "I wouldn't give her the drippings from my nose!" She was from East London/Essex.'

@chris_swan

'My dad used to say to us jokingly, "You great orme's head!" when we were being a bit gormless. I always thought he'd made it up until a day trip to Llandudno as an adult and there it was: the Great Orme headland in all its glory.'

@ascacupuncture

'Nan and family would call any nosy parker "aspidistra face". Nan said "aspadastra" as she struggled over some words (e.g. "delalerla sugar"). It was because some women when called out would claim they'd only been polishing their aspidistra leaves in the window and the curtain twitched.'

@lomquiche

More from the Rosen family. The Yiddish-English equivalent of 'Sticks and stones will break my bones (etc.)' uses the word 'pisher' – which literally means 'pisser' but in reality means a useless or weedy person. You say, 'So they call you pisher!' meaning, 'What's the worst that can happen to you?!'

Meanwhile, my mother would say, 'Who do you think you are? Lord Oomp?'

I've lived in London all my life and my parents too, apart from my father's first two years living in Brockton, Massachusetts. They were East Enders, my father living behind what is now the Royal London Hospital, my mother in Bethnal Green. By the time I knew them (!), we were living in the north-west suburbs and they had lost their East London accents and were teachers. Even so, they could both 'do' East End accents and my father in particular seemed to enjoy it.

It's said that rhyming slang originated in the chat of market traders and petty thieves, partly in order to disguise what it was they were saying. The problem with some rhyming slang is that it's hard to sort out whether they are words that were developed as part of 'street culture' or were invented as part of comedy routines, TV sit-coms and the like. Not that it matters!

My father often used the phrase 'dicky bird': 'It's amazing, Connie, I wrote to him months ago. Not a dicky bird.' (Meaning I haven't heard a word/dicky bird from him.)

The best rhyming slang words are the ones that seem to carry over some kind of meaning from the word they rhyme with. Here, it's as if the dicky bird should have spoken the word!

Friends at school used to say: 'Gissa butcher's', meaning 'give us a look'. I had no idea until much later that this came from 'butcher's hook/look'. Here's some more Cockney:

'Our mum, Olive Hornby, was born in 1908 in the East End and was a true Cockney. She passed away in 2006 but we remember her with such love and fondness, so much so that we have typed up all her old expressions. None of us are sure how many of these were generally used in the East End or were just "Olivisms".

- "You've got eyes like a stinking eel" (you see right through me)

- "I like to hear ducks fart" (you don't impress me)

- "She's a tit in a fit" (useless)

- "I've dropped my orange" (broken wind)

- "Look at the time, and no poes emptied" (running late)

- "I'm blown up like a poisoned pup" (I've overeaten)

- "If you can't fight, wear a big hat" (bluff your way out of it)

- "I've got the screws" (I've got arthritis)

Jennifer and William Barrett

2 7

If a teacher was coming when we were up to no good, we'd shout: 'Scarper!' This is a nice example of disputed origins.

Some say it comes from 'Scapa Flow' in the Orkneys, a famous base for the British fleet; others say it comes from the Italian 'scappare'. But because language is messy and not as neat and ordered as dictionaries, it's possible it came from both!

There was a young lad at my school who warned my friends that if I turned up at the bus stop at the bottom of the hill, there would be trouble. 'If Rosie's coming down the hill, tell him I'll bash his head in.' I got the message several times that 'Quozz' had this in mind for me. A few weeks later I did turn up at the bus stop. There was Quozz. There was me. We stood side by side at the bus stop, and after a while he said, 'Taters, innit?'

I nodded, pretending that I knew what he was talking about. He got on one bus, I got on another and that was the end of it. I've never seen him since. I did do some teenage research and found out that he was doing rhyming slang: 'taters in the mould/cold' ('taters' of course are potatoes). Why are taters in the mould? That's a reference to gardeners piling up earth as the potatoes reach ripeness, known as a mould. Of course, potatoes also go mouldy.

For some reason, the testicles of monkeys have attracted London speakers. 'It's brass monkeys' (as cold as taters, you'll find) is short for 'so cold it would freeze the balls off a brass monkey'.

Meanwhile 'I don't give a monkey's' means 'I don't care about it'. Which bit of the monkey being referred to here is disputed but the testicles are one candidate.

While we're on testicles, for some reason if something is very, very good, it's 'the dog's bollocks'.

I once interviewed a market trader in Hackney and he told me that if they knew that one of the punters was particularly stingy they called him Johnny Longpockets. He conjured up the scene of someone that he and his sons were familiar with who would come up to their fruit stall, pick up an orange or an apple, put it down, go to buy one, then change his mind and walk off. So when he was spotted, the trader would say to his son, 'Johnny Longpockets at a quarter past.' 'Quarter past' is like points on a compass taken from the hands on a clock.

Where the origins of June are clouded over, the origins of July are clear and simple. It's named after Julius Caesar. We might know of him through Shakespeare, the Asterix books or indeed the school rhyme:

> Julius Caesar
> The Roman geezer
> Squashed his nose
> In a lemon squeezer.

He was of course a real historical figure. In fact, he was so real that the Senate decided that he was a god, the same Senate that named his birth-month after him.

The phrase 'render unto Caesar what is Caesar's' doesn't come from Shakespeare but from the Bible – nor does it apply to Julius Caesar as he was dead by the time the historical Jesus lived. This leaves the person being referred to as either Caesar Augustus (the Caesar at the time of Jesus's birth) or Tiberius (the Caesar at the time of Jesus's death) or monarchy in general.

Shakespeare gives Caesar some great lines, but the real Julius Caesar seems to have come up with some memorable ones of his own:

– It is easier to find men who will volunteer to die, than to find those who are willing to endure pain with patience.

– I came, I saw, I conquered.

– Experience is the teacher of all things.

– If you must break the law, do it to seize power: in all other cases observe it.

If true, this gives us some sense of a man who was domineering, egotistical, ruthless and brutal. Presumably, that's why a chosen few (including me) sat week after week in Latin lessons translating Caesar's *Gallic Wars*. Perhaps we were supposed to absorb unknowingly Caesar's view of the world as we struggled with Latin grammar.

The most famous line that Shakespeare gives him is 'Et tu, Brute?' (Latin for 'And you, Brutus?'). It can be slightly disconcerting to hear this in the theatre because it comes after an hour or so of believing that the English everyone is speaking is really Latin. Then all of a sudden, you're hit with this memorable line in Latin. So what were they speaking before? (Not really the question you should be asking yourself at the very moment you're in the midst of the spectacle of Caesar being stabbed to death.)

Some other great lines that Shakespeare gave to Julius Caesar come in this speech:

Let me have men about me that are fat,
Sleek-headed men and such as sleep a-nights.
Yond Cassius has a lean and hungry look,
He thinks too much; such men are dangerous.

This has been interpreted as a Machiavellian view of governance: that rulers and leaders should want dozy, smarmy, yes-men around them, rather than hungry, thoughtful types. What a cynical suggestion!

Those of us who opted to learn Latin (or our parents opted for us) whiled away the time reciting faux Latin rhymes. In case you think there is some cunning meaning hiding behind these words, rest assured that the gag is precisely the opposite: there is no meaning, it's the sound of the words that make a kind of sense in English.

Caesar adsum iam forte
Brutus aderat
Caesar sic in omnibus
Brutus sic inat.*

Often forgotten, so let's remember it now, the great Julius Caesar invaded Britain twice – in 55 and 54 BC. One reason Caesar himself gave for trying was that the Britons were helping the Gauls. Others have suggested that he conducted a foreign war in order to win favour with the Roman people – a principle followed by many rulers since.

The first invasion force seems to have tried to land at or near Pegwell Bay in Ebbsfleet. Fun to think of the word 'July' having a biographical link to Ebbsfleet. The invasion was badly planned and it went downhill from there. By all accounts, Caesar and the army were lucky to escape.

The second time Caesar tried to invade, he was better prepared and arrived with some 27,000 troops. Again he and his army landed in Ebbsfleet and after a series of battles and treaties may well have reached Wheathampstead in Hertfordshire. Another place to connect to 'July'.

As with many invaders, Caesar had a view of the people he was attempting to subjugate:

> Most of the tribes living in the interior do not grow grain;
> they live on milk and meat and wear skins. All the Britons
> dye their bodies with woad, which produces a blue colour
> and gives a wild appearance in battle. They wear their hair
> long; every other part of the body, except for the upper lip,
> they shave. Wives are shared between groups of ten or twelve

---

* I'll spoil the joke by spelling it out: 'Caesar had some jam for tea. Brutus had a rat. Caesar sick in omnibus. Brutus sick in hat.'

men, especially between brothers and between fathers and sons; but the children of such unions are counted as belonging to the man with whom the woman first cohabited.

[Translation based on W.A. McDevitte and W.S. Bohn (1869)]

We might say of Caesar then that he came, he saw, he conquered (sort of) and left never to return, though we do invoke his name every time we say 'July'. Another form of conquering, perhaps.

I've always loved a malapropism, which is the accidental use of a word in place of a word that sounds the same, and they often give very funny results.

The word 'malapropism' is an eponym. (How many words about words can you squeeze into one sentence?) Mrs Malaprop is a character in Richard Sheridan's play *The Rivals* (1775). She misspeaks (done for comic effect by Sheridan), and since then, muddles and mispronunciations have been named after her. 'Malaprop' is a joke in itself. 'Mal à' in French means literally 'bad at' (although if you are 'mal à la tête', you've got a headache). The 'prop' bit of the name is a hint at 'appropriate' or 'proper'.

Here's one from my dad, albeit a deliberate one:

I went with some friends and my parents to Whipsnade Zoo. Every time we got to a sign that said, 'These animals are dangerous', my father said, 'See that sign? It says, "These animals are dangeroos".' (Rhyming with 'kangaroos'.) We tried to see where the dangeroos were.

Here's another. A friend of mine didn't say 'in one fell swoop'. He said (because he thought this was the proper expression), 'in one foul swipe'. And it works! 'He fired half the staff in one foul swipe.'

It turns out that many of you also have fond memories of your own family malapropisms:

'My family shared a love of mispronunciations or malapropisms – growing up in an unheated house in the 1960s, we often used to remark that the windows were "running with condescension".'

Linda Aird

'A friend's bubbe (granny) used to say she had to go and see her "physical terrapin" (physiotherapist!).'

Edwina Broadbent

'We inherited the phrase "octopus unusual" instead of optical illusion from my little sister (Vanessa). She thought that is what we had said and it stuck for ever more!'

@TamariskYoga

'My friend's late elderly mum blithely called decaffeinated coffee "defecated coffee".'

@Hoarder55

'A malapropism of my sister's that became a family favourite: "I wouldn't trust him with a bargepole."'

@angusdawalker

'A few years ago, when she was in her nineties, my late mum was telling us about the hairdressers in her small town. One in particular was a "bi-sexual business".'

@tjwitters

'Due to a mishearing by my daughter, we like to pick up bargains from a "tragedy shop".'

James Jacktosome Piercy

Sentenced to a sentence

Here's a tweet by the poet and broadcaster Ian McMillan: 'Fewer tweets today because Louie Louie's coming to play. Better get those diggers and tractors lined up! Come on grandad, let's improvise another digger and tractor song!'

When I think back to the way in which I was taught about language from about the age of ten to 23, it was mostly about sentences. The sentence was the king of language. We were told over and over again what a sentence is: it has a 'finite verb' in a 'main clause', and it begins with a capital letter and ends with a full stop, question mark or exclamation mark.

They told us very clearly what is a finite verb and what is a main clause. They also told us that there were several types of sentence: a statement, a question, a command and an exclamation. To identify these, they told us that the finite verbs are different. In a statement we write things like 'Michael is eating breakfast.' In a question, we write things like 'Is Michael eating breakfast?' In a command, we write, 'Eat your breakfast!' In an exclamation we write, 'What a breakfast Michael is eating!'

You'll notice that in each of these sentences, apart from the command, the 'eat' or 'is eating' part (the verb) has a someone doing the eating: Michael is the 'subject'. Other kinds of subjects can be 'pronouns' (like he, she, you, they etc.) or 'nouns' like 'cloud', 'buses', 'love'. A phrase can be a subject too, as in 'Hearing the car rev surprised me.'

The examples of sentences from two paragraphs up are all 'main clauses'. We were told that the other kind of clause were 'subordinate clauses': these have 'finite verbs' in them but begin with words like 'when', 'which', 'where', 'although', 'if', and many others. 'Michael is eating breakfast, <u>although he should be at work by now</u>.' The underlined words are a subordinate clause.

So the formula again: a sentence is a main clause with a finite verb in it, and it begins with a capital letter and ends with a full stop.

If we didn't write sentences, we were told: 'This is not a sentence.'

Now let's look at Ian's tweet.

First bit: 'Fewer tweets today because Louie Louie's coming to play.'

Capital letter – yes.

Full stop – yes.

Finite verb – yes in the bit that comes after 'because' ... 'Louie Louie [is] coming'.

But as it's in a 'because clause' (a subordinate clause), it's not in the main clause.

So where's the main clause?

Ah! There isn't one. The main 'bit' is 'Fewer tweets today'.

Now we probably read that as something like 'I'll be doing fewer tweets today' or 'There will be fewer tweets today' – but that's not what Ian wrote. So my teachers from 60 years ago would write, 'This is not a sentence. Where is the finite verb?'

But I can guess Ian doesn't care. In fact, I would also guess that Ian rather likes his 'Fewer tweets today'. It's snappy. It gets right to the heart of the matter. It's chatty too. I know Ian. It sounds just like him. Elsewhere in this book I've talked about how every bit of writing comes in a genre, with a topic and for an audience. This genre is 'the tweet', with a sub-genre of 'my news'. The topic is 'today'. The audience is the audience that Ian has built up of people who like his tweets about poetry, his family, his morning strolls, local culture. He has a cast list of characters, and Louie Louie is one of them. But 'grandad' (him) is often there with the grandchildren, playing football and other games.

This is a long way of saying that it's entirely appropriate that Ian has written a 'sentence' (or something like it) without a finite verb in this context.

But that's not what they taught me at school. This was slightly bizarre because skidding under the radar were things like dialogue in plays (including Shakespeare), or poems that, when added up, had hundreds of sentences without finite verbs in them.

There's one famous one elsewhere in this book: the extract about fog by Charles Dickens.

Playwrights often try to reproduce conversational language, in which we most certainly speak regularly without those finite verbs. How odd that we didn't write next to them, 'this is not a sentence'. That was because in the Land Where Sentence is King, it was not said that there were very good ways of speaking and writing without finite verbs.

We were sentenced to the sentence.

Just in case we might think that Ian has made a mistake with his first 'sentence', does he do it again with his next 'sentence'?

'Better get those diggers and tractors lined up!'

That's debatable. Is he giving himself a command? 'Get those diggers lined up!'

Or is he saying (without saying it): 'I had better get those diggers lined up'?

What do you think?

Will my teacher write, 'This is not a sentence' next to it, or will he get away with it?

You decide.

I love it when the strict categories for language don't look quite so watertight as they did when they were listed in our grammar books. I once had a minor tiff with a famous linguist about something that an England football manager said after the team had lost: 'It wasn't to be.'

It's a perfectly good thing to say. It's got a proverbial, almost biblical quality about it. But what does a grammarian make of it? After several hundred words of discussion, he wasn't sure. In the end he parked it in just the same place as we park idioms and proverbs: as complete phrases in themselves that we can't bust open with the usual grammatical terms. We say, for example: 'More haste, less speed'. It's a complete statement but – arrrggghhh – it has no finite verb. Should we drop it? Should I write next to it, 'This is not a sentence'? Or should I admire it for its poetic symmetry, its neat placing of one thing against another, its rhythm, its ability to convey a lot in just four words?

In truth, we surround ourselves with non-sentence sentences: newspaper headlines, proverbs, idioms, texts, social media posts, ads, film scripts, TV scripts, plays, poems, song lyrics and of course, every day, all day long in our conversations. Some of these areas are of huge commercial value:

thousands of people put in a huge amount of effort and time trying to get these non-sentences right – songwriters, ad copy-writers, scriptwriters.

Isn't it just a bit strange that we put 'the sentence' on a pedestal and the non-sentence sentence hardly gets a mention?

I've taken to collecting them. This is my most recent:

'No enterprise too big.

No entrepreneur too small.'

(Tube ad)

I love a non-sequitur, a sentence or word that doesn't logi-cally follow the one that came before. We often use them in awkward moments, and they can become family classics:

'My paternal grandmother used to say, "Chopin died when he was 39, you know," randomly in a conversation she wasn't interested in. It used to drive my dad crazy.'

@rednotgrey

'If someone comes out with something that's irrelevant or a non-sequitur, my dad would respond, as if in reply to a non-existent conversational thread, "I used to play cricket."'

@DaniellePezza

'A girlfriend of my brother's once came out with "My aunt-ie's had her hair cut" that was forever thereafter the family response to a non-sequitur/irrelevance.'

@spkenny67

'A non-sequitur we use: "That's the badger."'

@DoctorT1992

'"I'll sit on the commode" – an inherited family phrase from when my great-grandmother would have lots of family over at Christmas and – not having enough chairs for everyone – have to sit on the portable commode. It is now used anytime anyone feels they are begrudgingly taking the rubbish option so the rest of the family can have something better (e.g. having the end burnt piece of flapjack so everyone else can have a nice piece). It's always said with extra dramatic emphasis to show the sacrifice bestowed by the grand gesture.'

Chloe Hope

'One morning, my mother, my two sibs and I were all awake but quietly reading in our bedrooms. Suddenly we heard our mother say, "So, has anyone seen the grapefruit knife?", as if we'd been having a conversation about it. So in our family, a grapefruit knife is a non-sequitur.'

@LaurenceSarno

Now to the Midlands, where there's a rich seam of great sayings:

'My nan used to look after me in the school holidays. She was born 1902 in South Staffordshire, and these sayings are pure Black Country. She'd tell me to "Gerroff the ossrode and stay on the corsie" (get out of the horse road and stay on the causeway, i.e. pavement), and then to "Stay in the fode" (stay in the fold, which in this case was the walled back yard).'

Chris Ramsbottom

'This reminds me, during a neighbourly dispute, one of my husband's family went round theirs to remonstrate. When the door was answered by a youngster, she was told by an adult indoors to "shut the door in 'is ferce, little'un, if yo' dow are wull". It's now a saying with us.'

@brendarogers2

'My nan and great-auntie (born and bred in pre-WWI Black Country) would often say something that sounded like "Gu'tan!" as an expression of shock. Weirdly this was a shortening of 'Go to Hannover', a less blasphemous way of saying 'Go to hell.' Anyone else ever heard that?'

@DarkBlogMan1

'"I couldn't get me 'at on." It was a Brummie expression I used to use a lot. It means "I couldn't believe it."'

@EmmaFlowersBand

'My parents were from Staffordshire and would say, "Stop kiddeling on that chair."'

@BiddyBoo3

Some more Midlands expressions:

— 'Stop your blarting' is 'stop your crying'.

— 'Hotch oop' means 'move up'.

— 'I cuzn't' is 'I couldn't'.

— 'Ow bist?' is 'how are you?'

— 'Yow got a right cob on' – 'You're in a bad mood'.

— 'I coulda drapped cork-legged' – 'I was surprised'.

![21]

Cursing and swearing are part of who we are. Some people see them as the opening part of physical conflict but sometimes they're the opposite, words instead of deed.

I've heard some very creative alternatives to swearing, and I'll share those over the next few days. Let's start with one of mine. In the 1950s, where I lived (Pinner), other parents didn't swear but mine did, so my friends used to come over specially in order to hear my father swear: e.g. 'shit and bloody derision!' and 'scheiss Gesicht' (which I helpfully translated for them: 'shitface').

However, my mother censored my father's Yiddish swearing.

> Dad: 'Khaliera zolstu nimmen.'
> Mum: 'Don't say that!'
> Me: 'What did he say? What did he say?'
> Mum: 'Don't tell him, Harold!'

And now for some of yours:

'My mum (now 85) has always said "beanbags" rather than "bother", "drat" or alternatives. A teacher-training-college tennis partner said it, being short for: "Beanbags, Wendy houses and water play, and all the naughty words I'm not allowed to say."'

@clarinetRuth

'My mum's go-to curse was "hell's bells and buckets of blood".'

@LindsayE_A

'My grandmother would often exclaim "I'll spifflicate you!" if I was doing something naughty when I was small. It meant she wasn't really cross – it was a laughing threat of violence that was never carried through. My mother also used it, and so do I today.'

@JaqCole

'Arguably the best expression in the English language is said when someone looks at things that are none of their business: "Trunky wan' a bun?"' [Trunky – from sticking your 'trunk' in it – wants a bun]

@thepiercy

My friends at school had another 'trunk' expression. If you were nosey or barged in, they would say, 'Trunk out, Rosen,' which could be shortened to a gesture, holding your arm up to your nose and waving it about like an elephant's trunk.

What is the world's most famous curse?

One contender is one that took place on the field of play in the 2006 World Cup Final between France and Italy. The whole world (metaphorically speaking) is watching. Two players square up to each other, Zidane from France and Materazzi from Italy. Suddenly Zidane head-butts Materazzi. Zidane, one of the world's greatest footballers at the time, if not ever, is sent off.

The whole world (kind of) asks themselves, 'Why did he do it? What kind of provocation was so bad, so terrible that it would result in a great footballer head-butting another and throwing (or risking throwing) this huge sporting tournament?' At first no one knew, then one way or another, it's been revealed. If a defender stays very close to an attacker (as Materazzi was to Zidane), one joke that the attacker can say is, 'Do you want my shirt?' Zidane said this. How did Materazzi reply? He said, 'I prefer your sister.'

For that, a World Cup was lost.

Regarding that curse of my father's that I didn't understand, 'Khaliera zolstu nimmen.'

Years and years later I managed to get it out of my father that he was saying, 'May you catch cholera.'

What?

In Pinner in the 1950s, my father was uttering a curse from out of medieval Europe? How bizarre was that.

Not that I understood it. I didn't even know what cholera was, let alone understand the Yiddish.

The word 'bastard' has proved to be useful over many centuries whether as a factual description, something to be proud of (as with Edmund in Shakespeare's *King Lear*, who has the memorable line 'Stand up for bastards') or as a word of abuse. By the way, the prefix 'Fitz' on the front of a name – as with Fitzwilliam – means literally 'son' (from the French 'fils'). This could mean legitimate or illegitimate.

Cursing people for being illegitimate, or implying that they are, has long proved to be a potent insult. In Mandarin, the coded way to do that is to refer to eggs, in particular turtle eggs, as turtles are deemed to be promiscuous. The only word I know in Mandarin is the word for 'grandpa' but I will make sure that I avoid any mention of turtle eggs as it could sound as if I'm calling someone a bastard.

'My grandad, a gregarious character from Hull, used to begin speeches at family occasions by saying, "And may I be the first to dangle my balls in the custard." He's long passed but I'm looking forward to the day my daughter gets married.'

@CheKaye

Auguste

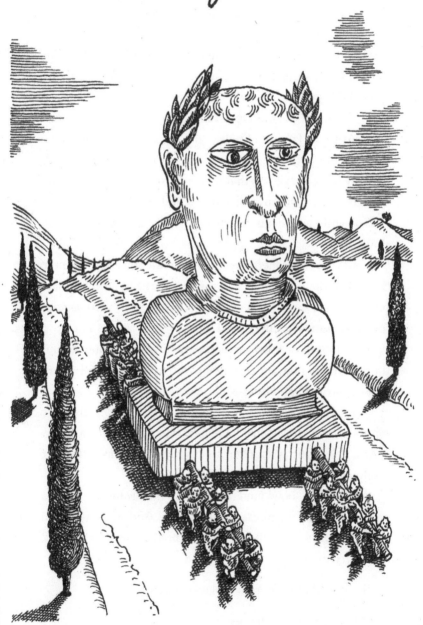

One interesting thing about August is that we pronounce it differently from the way we pronounce 'august'. To my mind this nearly makes it a heteronym. If I'm being a purist, a true heteronym is a word that has at least two meanings which are spelled the same way, AND look the same way, and – this is key – we pronounce them differently to indicate the difference. As we all know, in English (not in, say, French), we put a capital letter at the beginning of our names for months, that's why my personal view is that it 'nearly makes it a heteronym'. Another near heteronym like this is 'polish/Polish'.

So while we're on heteronyms, what others can you think of?

Some are heteronyms because the difference is due to the 'function' the word plays in the sentence. In grammatical terms, one is, say, a noun and the other is, say, a verb, as with 'object', 'suspect', 'intern' and 'reject'.

Other kinds of heteronym have meanings, pronunciations and functions that are completely different. Think of 'tear', 'close', 'present' and 'refuse'.

Some might surprise us if we isolate them on the page without any context, like 'analyses'. Here's how it's a heteronym: 'First our researcher analyses the data and then her analyses should reveal the truth.'

A word like 'bow' (and 'bows') can give us fun for quite a while, coming up with its different uses. And while we're on uses, don't forget that the uses can be used, if she uses the uses.

Or try these:

– 'I crooked my arm so it looked crooked.'

– 'I'll desert him in the desert.'

- 'She knows what does do, but does she know what a doe does?'

- 'The sign over the entrance will entrance you.'

- 'Are you trying to intimate you want to be intimate?'

- 'His claim to be an invalid was invalid.'

- 'I can lead you to the lead' and 'You can read what I read yesterday.'

- 'He moped about not having a moped.'

- 'A number of my fingers feel number today.'

- 'The unionised lab assistant handled the unionised solution.'

- And that old favourite: 'She wound the bandage round her wound.'

None of this has anything to do with why August is called August. Following on from Julius Caesar and July, August is named after a Roman ruler – the Emperor Augustus, who was Julius Caesar's nephew. In fact, Augustus was a name he was given later in life. He was born Gaius Octavius in 63 BC but became Gaius Julius Caesar Augustus or even Imperator (Emperor) Caesar Augustus.

The word 'augustus' at that time seems to have indicated that he was much revered, perhaps both politically and religiously. That's to say, he was so great, he became divine. How do you become divine, if you're a Roman ruler? By conquering vast tracts of land. Augustus was credited with leading the Roman army to conquer territories that we now know of as Spain, Portugal, Switzerland, Bavaria, Austria, Slovenia,

Albania, Croatia, Hungary, Serbia, Tunisia, Egypt, Israel and the Occupied Territories, and parts of Algeria, Libya and Syria. Historians have noticed that Augustus was at war in each and every year between 30 BC and AD 14. This meant that for around 45 years he was out and about fighting wars somewhere or another.

It was in 27 BC that Gaius Octavius was given the name Augustus and then, in 8 BC, the month of Sextilis was renamed in his honour as Augustus. This was probably because of his greatest conquests, especially that of Egypt which was conquered in and around August. As with Julius Caesar, when we say the name of the month, we find ourselves unknowingly memorialising Roman imperial ambition.

No one knows for certain how Augustus died. It's possible he was killed by his wife Livia, with poisoned figs, though the same method could have been suicide by agreement between the couple. His last words were, supposedly, 'Acta est fabula, plaudite', which translates loosely as, 'The play is over – applaud!'

I guess this is a literal example of what we mean when we say that someone is 'self-dramatising'.

We received some sayings from north and north-west England.

'Here are some from my Sheffield upbringing: "mardy bum" (sulky), "dolly-posh" (left-handed), "over old Bill's mother" (yonder) or "more (whatever) than soft Mick".'

@davidhillatilc

3

'Growing up in West Yorkshire, I was often asked to "siden the table", meaning to clear it. Or: "Side them pots for us." If a big cleaning session was required: "This house needs a reyt good side-ation."'

@TitaLulah

4

'Wonky = "ont' soss" is similar from South Yorkshire, according to my former miner of an uncle. His mum, who was a seamstress, also used it when something was badly stitched or assembled, when she would say it was "cut ont' soss".'

@poor_n_stained

5

'"Put the door on the sneck" meaning to push that little button on the Yale lock so it doesn't lock when you close the door (West Riding of Yorkshire).' ['Sneck' also meant nose in West and South Yorkshire.]

@Roseberrykate

6

'A local word I like a lot is "oining" – to annoy or mither (Bacup in East Lancashire).'

@Dr_David_James

7

'From Halifax: Mum (b. 1927) would say "got to keep t'band in t'nick" when referring to having to keep something going smoothly, e.g. going to work (to earn money) or doing some tedious but essential task.

It's an old industrial reference from the textile mills, I gather: the band was the cord nested in the nick or groove of the wheel or spindle that drove the machinery. The phrase was already long detached from its origins and in general use when my mum acquired it.'

Ruth Bourne

'Wigan dialect: "By the roastin' crin!" – roughly equivalent to "Blinking 'eck."'

Carol Anne Whinnom

Another of Carol Anne's expressions was a response that many listeners sent in:

'"It fevvers a pea on a drum" – that person's hat is too small for their head.'

'"Get out road, tha' weren't made in St Helen's" – "You are standing in my light so I can't see. Please move." St Helen's is where the Pilkington glass factory was.'

Carol Anne Whinnom

'If I asked my Lancastrian father to explain something and he deemed it none of my business, he'd say it was "layholes for meddlers". It seems "layhole" is a dialect term for a grave.'

@StockportDiesel

'Apologies to any Cumbrians with the spelling here but I only had my grandfather's voice for them. A "gadgy" was a person. "Bari" meant good. Therefore a "gadgybari" was a good person. All pretty clear if you ask me.'

@kingvagabondHOL

Lancashire: 'Dun yew a thickun?' (Have you messed up?)

Another from Lancashire: 'When it comes to ey lads ey.' (When it comes down to the real world.)

Noggins
The scene is as follows:

There is a big hole in the floor. A builder has made the hole. The hole is in the floor of our house. We are looking into the hole. In some houses we would be looking into a cellar but in this house it's just the space between the floorboards and ground, a space that we hardly ever think about. In old houses like ours, to look into this space is to look into history: it's the archaeology of how the house came to be built. It may even give you a glimpse of the land before it was settled and built as a London street.

The reason we're all looking into the hole is because we want to know if the house has foundations. I'm not sure why we need to know this, but I'm someone who takes what builders say as fact, even though this has often ended up in disaster. I'm not just a slow learner on this. I'm a reluctant learner – or a school refuser, more like. I keep on believing that all builders are telling me facts. Often they do. Sometimes they don't.

Back with hole. The builder shines a torch. About three or four feet below us is a flat surface. I think of it as the 'ground'. But it's not naked earth, which round here is London clay. I can see that it's not London clay. It's flat and dark, some parts darker than others. The builder nods knowingly. 'Blinding,' he says. For a moment, I think it's an exclamation. 'Blinding!' Perhaps he's going to say 'Terrific!' or 'Fantastic!' too. Then he explains that when the house was built, they didn't make a concrete 'pad' and build the house on that as they would do today. What they did was break up bricks or stones and hammer them flat into an impacted hard surface.

I take this in. I repeat it in my head: 'blinding, blinding'. Why haven't I heard that word before? My parents renovated three old houses. I had been in on the conversion of two houses before this one. Maybe I hadn't been paying attention. As it happens, I had got used to this builder saying things that were new to me. He seemed to have a vast vocabulary of words I had either never heard before or had forgotten. People familiar with this lingo will know that he didn't use the word 'foundations'. He said 'footings'.

Why would that be? Why would we have some kind of 'standard' word for things that houses are built on but the people who make the thing in question have another? I would be more than happy to call 'foundations' the 'footings' but in my mouth it feels artificially artisan, as if I'm a skilled trades-man. You may also have noticed that the word 'foundation' has its origins in French and Latin, but the word 'footings' has its origins in Old English. Do these two words represent what was once the structure of English society? After 1066, the ruling order was Norman. They spoke Norman French. Those being ruled spoke Old English (a set of dialects owing their origins to the peoples who settled in Britain from what is now the Netherlands, Belgium, Germany, Denmark, Norway, Sweden and Iceland). Was this old structure being played out as I and the builder stared into the hole under our house?

He wasn't done. He jumped down onto the blinded surface (see how easily I popped the word in?), shone the torch and said, 'Corbelling.' To be fair to myself, this one rang a bell. As part of the obligatory walks that my parents demanded of my brother and me when we were growing up, there were the visits to look at ancient stuff. My father would pore over the Ordnance Survey map and call out words like 'tumulus'. Four or five hours later, after some heavy walking over boggy fields and moors, we would arrive at a mound and my father would say again, 'Tumulus!' And said with pride too. The corbel-ling bit would happen inside some other kinds of ancient pile, stones laid on top of each other so as to create a sloping support for a roof. In the same manner of his tumulus shout, my father would point at a ceiling in a cold damp place, say, 'Corbelling!' and we would walk on for another ten miles.

'Corbelling?' I said to the builder. He demonstrated with his hands and explained that the bricks at the bottom of the house were laid on top of each other so that they widened out into a base. Underneath the house in that usually invisible space, the walls at the very bottom ended in little steps: 'sitting on the blinding' as the builder put it.

Now there was a thought. What was preventing the house from sinking into the London clay was corbelling and blinding. A few bricks laid on top of each other in step formation and a layer of smashed and pounded bricks and stone beneath it. Is this enough? I wondered. I asked the builder. 'It's not going anywhere,' he said. I recognised this bit of builder talk. In principle, it's fine. Houses don't go anywhere. Usually. But I could tell you a story of how … no, I won't.

I'll just leave you with a couple of other builder words. Not that I'm an expert – far from it – but there's a thing I call a 'cornice'. Any stretch of plaster fitted into the angle between a wall and ceiling, I call a cornice. Not so, builders. If it's plain and straight, they call it 'coving'. If it's decorated, they call it a cornice. Mostly. But not always. In fact, one builder (not the blinding, corbelling one) did something amazing. The cornice (and this one was a cornice) was a highly decorated, floral affair but damaged. He explained that it was made in pieces, each one about nine inches long. Cornice-makers made moulds and turned out enough for each house. He said that across London, say, there are hundreds of different designs – flowers, fruit, arches or whatever. He said he had a collection of moulds that he had made but that he would have to make a new one for this bit of cornice. Which he did. He turned out a set of them and fitted them so that there was the old and the new cornice. By the way, this cornice-maker and fitter was not only very Dickensian in the way he talked – perhaps a bit like Wemmick in *Great Expectations* – but he read Dickens and would quote bits of it to me.

Up in the attic, back with the blinding, corbelling builder, we discussed whether it would be OK to store things there. He said that it would be best to put in some noggins. 'Right,' I said. Noggins? What would noggins be? I thought. Bolts? Brackets? Struts? Braces? Trusses? Joists? (See, I do know some builder words.) I nodded, hoping that noggins would come clearer in a moment. I did also think of *Noggin the Nog*, that old and very wonderful Oliver Postgate animated show on BBC children's TV but I did know Oliver and you only have to say 'Clanger' or 'Ivor' and I think 'Oliver!' My mind drifted off into thinking of someone who could be called Oliver Noggins.

Noggins are indeed a kind of strut or support that builders can wedge in the angle of beams or rafters to strengthen the structure. Again, I'm sounding like I know what I'm talking about. I don't. But I've got the words. No, I've got some words. No, I've got a tiny, tiny selection of builder words. And I often think how though both the builders and I can say those words, when I'm saying them, they have no attachment to my hands or body. They just float about in speech or in writing as I'm doing here. When the builders say them, they're attached to making, fitting, mending or working with the very things that the words name.

Language then creates a strange equivalence. Just as money buys things that are completely different – a bar of chocolate, a train ticket, the work it takes for a barber to cut my hair – language can seem on the surface as if it's doing the same. The builder and I can both name a noggin. But beneath the surface, the words (or is it us?) are doing very different things.

A Rosen family phrase: on the French-Spanish border, Le Perthus, 1953. Bloke jumps out of a Morris Minor in white shirt, khaki shorts and long socks and shouts in a posh voice, 'Does anyone round hee-ah (here) speak English?' For years after, my bro and I used to say it just as we would get out of the car for any holiday anywhere.

'My father-in-law used to say, "Don't get confused by the colour of the fireman's socks" when Philip was trying to solve a problem but was focusing on the thing that wasn't important.'

Gillie Stoneham

'If you were frustrated by something, you "could bite a nail in half".'

Charlotte Norman

'My mum on grafitti: "Fools' names are like their faces – always found in public places."'

Ed Igleheart

'My stepfather: "When a girl finds she isn't the only pebble on the beach, she becomes a little bolder."'

Another great example from Ed Iglehart

One of my own from the Rosen household.

> Mum: 'This lettuce is getting a bit old. I'll cheer it up.'
> (Puts lettuce in a bowl of water.)

'I'll cheer it up' has now become my go-to for any recycling of stale food by toasting it, or heating it, etc.

'We had to be "Bs up to the Cs" (bellies up to the counter) at lunch, and if we had visitors and weren't sure that there was enough to go round, it was "FHB": family hold back. Both were my dad's, learned from his mum in South London.'

Maggie Harbour

'In southern USA (where my mother grew up), tall, thin women like her were referred to as "six foot of picket fence".'

Lisa Brown

Snobberies

This page is pointless.

Many people like to look down on the way others speak. Sometimes linguists make strenuous efforts to point out that most of this is about some kind of social sneering or snobbery and that it has very little or nothing to do with some kind of objective fact. However, all that effort by well-meaning linguists (and me!) seems to have no effect. People will insist on objecting to the ways other people speak. It seems as if many people find it difficult to live with the idea that the way we produce language is varied and that with very little effort we could simply sit back and accept variation.

Here's Gerard Manley Hopkins's tribute to variation and diversity:

> Glory be to God for dappled things –
>> For skies of couple-colour as a brinded cow;
>> For rose-moles all in stipple upon trout that swim;
> Fresh-firecoal chestnut-falls; finches' wings;
>> Landscape plotted and pieced – fold, fallow, and plough;
>> And áll trádes, their gear and tackle and trim.
>
> All things counter, original, spare, strange;
>> Whatever is fickle, freckled (who knows how?)
>> With swift, slow; sweet, sour; adazzle, dim;
> He fathers-forth whose beauty is past change:
>>> Praise him.

Another poet, John Keats, asked us to think about 'negative capability'. He used the phrase in a letter to his brothers George and Thomas on 22 December 1817:

> Negative Capability, that is, when a man is capable of being in uncertainties, mysteries, doubts, without any irritable reaching after fact and reason ...

I take it from Hopkins and Keats that there are times or situations which we can accept as various. I'm all for reason and logic but when it comes to language – which, after all, is an aspect of human behaviour, not a mathematical calculation – we should expect variation. Two or more variations can be both right, rather than either right or wrong.

I know of several ways to say 'I am not': 'I amn't' (as heard in Ireland), 'I ain't' (heard all over the English-speaking world), 'I'm not' (likewise), 'I ent' (likewise). More locally, there are versions like 'me not', and quite often people say 'am not' without the 'I'. Millions of people every day are making these ways of speaking work. Many of these people will use several of them in any different day or week. Someone who says 'ain't' most of the time may well say 'I am not' if they're being very emphatic or vehemently denying something. It's not only that we are various between people; we are also various within ourselves.

As I was writing this page, someone explained to me on social media that they can't stand the 'glottal stop'. Let's think this one through. In a word like 'got', we 'stop' the vowel-sound 'o' with what we call a consonant. We write 't'. There is no rule, no deity that states how this 't' sound should be said. What happens is that communities of speakers and listeners create a kind of mutual acceptance about it. Three sounds that such communities make and accept are a 'd' sound (particularly with North American speakers), a 't' sound similar to the beginning of 'Tom', and the 'glottal stop', a sound we make at the back of our mouths. Phoneticians (who study this much more precisely than I'm doing here) have detected others.

Now let's remember that in the history of language, speech came before writing. If human behaviour is anything to go by, we should expect variation to have been in the making of language right from the beginning. The very idea of the prolif-eration of languages and dialects tells us this, so why should we expect conformity and uniformity within one language? Apart from anything, it's extremely hard, if not impossible, to determine a hard and fast difference between 'dialect' and 'language'. The famous quote is that a language is a dialect with an army and a navy. In other words, it's only when we attach the names of nation states to a dialect (or a dialect to a nation state) that it becomes a language. Flemish, Dutch and Afrikaans would be similar enough to be one 'language' with one name, if the speakers were living in the same country.

So back with the glottal stop. The person writing said that they couldn't stand the glottal stop. But if people can make it do the job of helping make words make sense, then the only objection can be that the very sound itself is attached to people who are being disapproved of. It's not the sound that is objectionable, it's the people making it. Sometimes this sort of thing is buttressed and supported by this or that thing: 'instead of saying "t" they say the glottal stop'. This is really a historical comment, which assumes that 't' came first and the glottal stop came lumbering along afterwards. Do we know that for certain? And if someone could prove it (I'm not sure how), and if it's been around for hundreds of years, that particular bit of history is no more an obstacle than that we write 'night' but don't say 'nicht'. Some people think that it's possible that Old English and Norman French said it one way and it was the Scandinavians (Vikings, Danes) who liked glottals.

By the way, even people who say they don't like glottal stops often say them themselves! Try listening to yourself or to others saying something like 'I've got ten of them'. Maybe you pronounce the 't' on the end of 'got' in exactly the same way as you pronounce the 't' at the beginning of 'ten', but mostly we don't. Many of us pop in a little glottal before we get to the 't' of ten. Just saying.

And so to 'aitch/haitch'. What a sad state of affairs that people should condemn others for the way they say this. Is there any problem in understanding what people mean when they say either one or the other? I also see that there are some spurious reasons around for justifying one way of saying it over the other.

Again, let's remind ourselves of something: the way we speak English is made up of many sources. The two main ones are Old English (as spoken by the migrants who came to these islands from the territories surrounding the east end of the 'English Channel' and the North Sea) and the other being the Norman French from Normandy, as spoken by the people we call the Normans. This mix broadly involved people combining 'Germanic' ways of speaking with 'Romance' ways of speaking (derived from Latin). I say 'broadly' because by the time the Norman arrived in 1066, Old English people had absorbed into their speech and writing quite a few words derived from Latin. And another complication: the history of Normandy and the Normans tells us that it was settled by Vikings, who originally arrived in Normandy speaking a Scandinavian Germanic language. Nothing is neat and simple about the history of languages.

If you know any French, you'll know about words beginning with 'h'. A bean is a 'haricot' which is pronounced something like 'urri-co' (southern British pronunciation). No breathy 'h' spoken at the beginning. Same goes for all the other French 'h' words.

Now, think of English 'h' words that might have been spoken by Norman French people when they came to England and throughout Britain. Here are some: habit, host, hospital. Linguists think that Norman French people didn't pronounce the 'h' in these words but, over time, people living in Britain started to. (Why the change? Who decided?) But of course there are exceptions. There always are. Like 'hour' and 'honour'.

Meanwhile, many people all over the English-speaking world don't pronounce the 'h' at the beginning of, say, 'horrible'. Sometimes I don't. I often say something like: 'That's orrible.' Perhaps such people have carried on with the French way of saying those words?

Note another snobbery: some people say that saying orri-ble or appy (happy) is bad. In which case, 'hour' and 'honour' are bad too! Meanwhile, 'haitch' is just as bad. Apparently.

This tells us that the 'h' is a 'site' of variation. In some people's speech they make an 'h' sound where in writing there is no 'h'. Sir Lenny Henry used to represent this in his sketches when imitating some older people from the Caribbean. He meant it affectionately but it can be a form of kicking down. I repeat: the 'h' is a site of uncertainty and variation.

Back to aitch/haitch again. Why has it happened that groups of people over time have stuck with haitch? Perhaps because saying the 'h' reminds people that's the sound they make when they see the letter? If so, that's quite handy. In Ireland, it has been a sign that demarcated Protestants and Catholics. People like markers that include themselves and exclude others.

Another is that there are two or more roots to the name of the letter anyway. The older one derived from Latin (and earlier) is an 'utch' sound (southern British pronunciation) and a later French name 'hache' pronounced 'ush' (southern British pronunciation). In fact, 'hache' in French today means both 'hatchet' or 'axe' and is also the name of the letter. Do you think the letter 'h' looks anything like an axe? I'll leave that thought with you.

Let's imagine the medieval French-speaking classes writ-ing 'hache' for the letter 'h', but saying it as 'ush' just as they wrote 'habit' but didn't pronounce the 'h'. Meanwhile people of all backgrounds start pronouncing the 'h' in most of the 'h' words (though not 'hour' and 'honour').

Don't we have a scenario then for people to vary in how they pronounce 'hache'? And later (with a vowel change) as 'aitch' and 'haitch'? The French French in France (if you get me) go on writing it as 'hache' and pronouncing it as 'ush'.

But, let's run with both aitch and haitch, so long as people want to say either or both. It really is no big deal. In fact, we can enjoy it, as Gerard Manley Hopkins might have said.

'My mum and her mum used to hurry us up by saying, "Come on, you're like one o'clock half struck."'

Bob Archer

This is technically the height of summer, so if you're in England, it's probably raining. But, hey, I'll pretend you're 'roasting', or 'sweating cobs' (cobbles? bread rolls?).

From Adrian Littlejohn – and many others who answered in a similar vein:

'If there was a small break in a cloudy sky, my gran would say, optimistically, that there was "enough blue sky to make a Dutchman a pair of trousers". Some people say: "Enough blue sky to make a sailor a suit." And there are other versions: "Is there enough blue sky to make a cat a pair of trousers?"

'If there was, then it would brighten up and stop raining, as the old man in charge of the weather had let the clouds out enough that he couldn't gather them back together again.'

'It's hotter than Dutch love' is said in Pennsylvania.

'Phew, it'll burn your bum off!' (if you go out in weather as hot as this).

There was a tradition in American party-pieces and entertainments to do 'it was so ...' jokes. Hot weather was one excuse for these:

— It was so hot that cows were giving evaporated milk.

— It was so hot that I saw a robin dipping his worm in iced tea.

— It was so hot that I saw a pigeon walking in the shadow of a fat man.

— It was so hot the hens were laying hard-boiled eggs.

A useful one for global warming: 'It's hotter than a jalapeño's armpit.'

(Do jalapeños have armpits? They do for the purposes of this joke.)

'Hot' can of course be used as a metaphor, as with 'he talks a lot of hot air', and also as a high approval rating for jazz or for someone who looks sexually attractive. There's an irony to this, given that heat can make us inactive, if not inert.

September

For anyone who knows Latin or any of the languages that have Latin origins, there's clearly a problem with September. The 'Sept' part of the name means seven but it's the ninth month in the year. This is not a mistake on account of someone ancient not being able to count but is due to the fact that, in the old Roman calendar, it was indeed the seventh month, in a year that began with March.

The Romans devoted a good deal of energy in September to playing games ('ludi') and celebrating the vine. Visually, September could be represented by a nude male wearing nothing more than a scarf (why not?), carrying a bunch of grapes and dangling a lizard on a string, an image that had something to do with Dionysus, or Bacchus as the Romans called him, the god of wine.

Two millennia later – on 19 September 1819, to be exact – the poet John Keats went for a walk near Winchester in Hampshire, along the River Itchen. He was so struck by what he saw and felt that the day spurred him on to write 'To Autumn', which famously begins:

> Season of mists and mellow fruitfulness,
>   Close bosom-friend of the maturing sun;
> Conspiring with him how to load and bless
>   With fruit the vines that round the thatch-eves run

With that hint of Dionysus in the last line, we could speculate whether Keats really did see grapes round the eves of thatched cottages near Winchester, but of course it's more than possible. However, with the warming of the planet, we know that if Keats were able to take a walk in Hampshire in September now, he would most certainly be able to set eyes on plenty of grapes, as it's become a centre for wine growing in England.

According to the Venerable Bede, September was known as the 'Holy Month' (Hāliġmōnaþ or Hāliȝmōnaþ) in Old English, before the Christian conversion and the adoption of Roman terms. However, it was also observed in an old poem that it was called the Holy Month on account of it being the time when the pre-Christian heathen ancestors had made sacrifices to their idols. So not 'holy' in the Christian sense, then.

September opens the show in the rhyme we use to remember how many days there are in each month. However, as with all mnemonics, if you can't remember the rhyme, it's not much use to you, as this reminds us:

Thirty days hath September,
All the rest I can't remember.

Big appetites are a thing we notice about each other.

So, how many ways are there to say that we are hungry? Here are a few:

'You've lost your appetite and found a donkey's.'

Jackie Turnbull

'My granny (only ever left Scotland once in her life) would say, "Ma moo is shapit for it", "shapit" being the local pronunciation and spelling of the past participle of shape (the "a" sound remains the same).'

@WiseShaz

'My mother used to say, "My moo is shap-ed for it." (My mouth is shaped for it, or I'm hungry for it … whatever it was).'

@VonnyRobby

'One from my mum, a never-ending source of linguistic delight. If she was very hungry, she'd say, "I could eat a tater more than a pig."'

@MaryMcKnight1

One from the Rosens. At the sight of a nice spread of food, my dad said, 'Shnobra-gants.' He said his zeyde (grandad) used to say it, but my father didn't know what it meant. Yiddish-ists have told me 'shnobra' is slang for nose/beak, 'gants' is a goose. So perhaps it means, I feel like geese do when they see food and flap their wings and honk.

'My grandad (North Yorkshire) always used to say, "Get it down yer Scalby Beck" to mean "finish your dinner". A form of rhyming slang I think was unique to him.

We say "get it down your Billingham Beck" here in the North East, meaning "get it down your neck". That or "Billy Beck".'

@A_Whyte73

Another Rosen phrase. Nosh (from Yiddish) can now mean 'food' (and a bawdy meaning too!) but when I was a kid, it meant some kind of food that was a treat, e.g. at the end of a meal.

Dad (after a huge meal): 'Is there any nosh?'

He was meaning some chocolates or chocolate biscuits.

In contrast to my father, I say after a big dinner, 'Anyone fancy a bowl of warm lard?'

'When my lad was little he logically presumed that, if food/drink could be off, it could also be on. Made total sense to us so we've adopted the phrase. To this day, we still ask, "Does this smell on to you?"'

Lisa Nelson

Synaesthesia – it's not what you say, it's the way that you say it

Let's start with the idea that there isn't anything 'tabley' about the word 'table'. After all, Germans call it a 'Tisch' and in Javanese it's 'meja'. In other words, there is nothing essentially table-like about these words. Human beings have created sequences of sounds ('phonemes') to signify stuff – things, ideas, feelings, processes, as well as grammatical words like 'to' or 'the' or 'would' to help us link the whole lot into meaningful sequences, but, we say, these sounds have nothing whatsoever to do with the things they describe. That's one theory.

Ah yes, but we make other sounds that have meaning but which are attempts by us to imitate the thing they name: 'moo', 'splash', 'plonk', 'cough' (onomatopoeia). And there are others that seem almost to mock this very attempt at imitation, as when we say, 'kerching!' to mean 'He made a load of dosh out of that bit of work', with an implication that there might even have been something dodgy about it. Or what do you make of a word like 'bling' to mean flashy jewellery? Does the flashiness make you 'bling' (whatever that might mean) – with a hint of the idea of 'blink'?

This reminds us that sometimes the sounds of words seem to fit the thing they're describing without being directly onomatopoeic. Poets have been playing with this for centuries through alliteration and assonance (playing with the repetition of consonant and vowel sounds through repetition). When we see things that we wonder about or are amazed by, we often say, 'Ah!' One famous poem we know about wondering begins:

Twinkle twinkle little star,
How I wonder what you are.

Can we say that the 'ar/are' sound on the end of those two lines imitates the 'ah' sound (in a southern British accent)?

There are thousands of examples from world literature where writers have tried to imitate whispering, rage, the sound of the waves, wind, hateful thoughts and much more, through words that are not directly onomatopoeic.

At school we said that these words 'have the effect of' indicating anger or sadness or some such but this always sounds to me too certain. We need to be more cautious about it and talk of 'hints' and 'possibilities' – and often it turns on how the actor or reader says the line.

When Macbeth says that 'tomorrow and tomorrow and tomorrow creeps in this petty pace from day to day', an actor may or may not hit 'petty pace' and 'day to day' in imitation of the rhythm of one day after another, like a metronome.

But again, we can say that surely 'petty', 'pace' and 'day' aren't words that sound like the things they're describing: smallness, movement, a section of time? It's the patterning of the words that gives us this hint of sound in meaning and meaning in sound.

Well, that's all very tidy. We've created some categories: the arbitrary way in which the signs we've created don't signify through their sound; the exceptions through onomatopoeic words; the exceptions when we create meaningful sound sequences.

But what if we look very closely at patterns of language? What if we found clusters of sounds (phonemes) that seem to cluster around words with similar meanings? When we say the 'b' sound at the beginning of a word, we close off the escape of air from our mouths, we activate our vocal folds, build up a bit of pressure behind the apparatus blocking off the escape (our lips) and then release the whole lot in one go: lips open, the air travels over our vocal folds and bursts out to make 'b'. In fact, I used the word 'burst', which, hey, begins with 'b'. As does 'begin'. And the onomatopoeic 'bang'. When I was about ten, we got an ad through our door which advertised 'Britain's biggest bunker bargain'. I walked round the house saying it over and over again. The ad worked insofar as it caught my attention. We didn't buy a new bunker though. Why did the company string those 'b' words together? Why did they think that they could sell more coal bunkers by doing that? I might guess that it's because they thought it was 'catchy', that the 'explosion' of the 'b' words would tickle people's senses in some way. Could 'big' have grown up to mean 'big' because people wanted to express something big through the sound (and the way we make the sound)? Certainly, 'big' is a word that is easy to use if you want to catch people's attention. But it isn't a big word, and it doesn't necessarily or always sound big.

But back with the clusters. What kinds of clusters have linguists spotted? I'll just say here that linguists write very serious, analytic articles about such things. One is called 'The Submorphemic Conjecture in English: Towards a Distributed Model of the Cognitive Dynamics of Submorphemes' by Didier Bottineau. What follows comes largely from his research. Merci, Didier.

That said, it's a lovely game to play yourself, whether you're just thinking of words or if you want to write a poem or a speech.

Let's start where Didier starts: with 'sp'. (If you want to shut your eyes and think of 'sp' words, go ahead!)

Didier picks: spin, span, spill, speak, spew, spit, spend, speck, spot, spate, spall, spawn, spook, spool, spam and spoon. At the ends of words: clasp and wisp; and separated in: sip, seep, sap, soap and soup. And then in another category: spray, sprawl, sprinkle, spring and sprightly.

What do you think links these words at the level of meaning (semantics)?

This is where it gets both complicated and (using Didier's word) full of 'conjecture'. He identifies 'centrifugal rotation', 'projection' and, in the case of that last sequence, beginning with 'spray', he talks of 'agentivity'.

So, over to you: do you think there is a sufficiently strong link between these 'sp' words (and 's-p' and '-sp' words) and a cluster of meanings? If you don't, then the conjecture can end. If you do, this has enormous significance. It suggests that sometime far back when humans started devising sounds to signify meanings, they did match some sounds (at the very least) to the things they described.

Didier goes on with 'st', 'sk', 'wr', 'sw', 'tw', 'cl', 'gl', 'sl'. He also has some detailed analysis of exactly where and how we produce these sounds with our tongues, teeth, lips and the roof of our mouths.

You can have fun with these.

Try 'gl', for example: 'glisten', 'glow', 'glimmer' 'glitter' and 'glint'. And does 'glory' glitter a bit? And do we 'glow' when we are 'gleeful'? Is 'glass' a bit 'glittery', does it 'gleam'? 'Glamour' is quite glittery, isn't it? Any more? 'Glide'? Maybe not. 'Glum'? No.

'Sl' is quite famous in the world of sub-morphemic conjecture. Didier is quite abstemious with his list here, so what can we come up with, including his?

Let's start with: sling, slug, slot, slay, slap, slate, sleet, sloop, slope, slide, slip, slake (Midlands dialect), sleek, slew.

And what semantic 'field' might you want to match to these? Some kind of movement, or the movement of the hands or hands imitating features around us, as with slope and sleet? Could we add 'sleep' because we lie down to sleep? Did our ancestors say the 'sl' sound at the same time as moving their hands and so started to distinguish between, say, slinging a stone, slaying an animal, indicating a slope, sliding along and lying down to go to sleep, and so on?

All this is called synaesthesia because it involves different processes at the same time: the sense of the object or process or thought, linked directly to the sound of the word, as with, say, the sight of something and the sound of the word.

Now to the West Country, and some of its best sayings:

'My dad used to say to us as kids after bathing, "Dry yourself properly, we don't want you to spreve." Spreve apparently meant to get sore or to get a rash.'

@jamm3roo

'One I have picked up teaching in Bristol: "Where we to?" 'It can mean all sorts of things: where we going? How are you? What page are we on? What room are we in? Where are we meeting?'

@neileley

'Cheers, drive!' (You say this to the bus driver as you get off.)

In Bristol, there's the lovely 'end-l' that people like to say on the ends of words. 'That's a good ideal' is 'that's a good idea'.

In Bath, you smooth the cat, rather than stroke it.

Around Dartmouth in Devon, people have been heard to greet each other with 'Hello, mackerel!'

Around Totnes, some locals say, 'It's good dryth', meaning it's good drying weather for wet clothes.

The BBC article 'Devon Dialect: Your Words and Phrases' has some Devon expressions, compiled by John Germon.

Trevor James from Tavistock offered 'a rantacket of a catchpenny', meaning a rip-off.

From the same BBC article for Devon dialect, Phil Tonkins wrote: 'I remember my grandfather saying to me the nimle-gang was giving him socks, meaning a whitlow (abscess) was giving him a lot of pain.'

Secret strings

Listen, children:
Your father is dead.
From his old coats
I'll make you little jackets;

I'll make you little trousers
From his old pants.
There'll be in his pockets
Things he used to put there,
Keys and pennies
Covered with tobacco;
Dan shall have the pennies
To save in his bank;
Anne shall have the keys
To make a pretty noise with.
Life must go on,
And the dead be forgotten;
Life must go on,
Though good men die;
Anne, eat your breakfast;
Dan, take your medicine;
Life must go on;
I forget just why.

This is a poem by Edna St Vincent Millay.

If you're interested in the 'how' of the poem, you can play the 'secret strings' game that I mentioned on page 87.

What we do is draw the 'strings' between any words or images that are linked in any way with any other. These can be repetitions, similarities or contrasts. We don't have to worry whether the writer put these links in deliberately. This is about how we read. Any link that we think is a link is a link, so long as we can justify it. I might find some links. You might others. You can't be wrong: there are just different ways of being right. When I use the word 'link' I'm talking of a 'secret string'.

My first link is from the word 'children' to 'Anne' and 'Dan'. Children is the general, Anne and Dan are the specific children. Then if I look through the poem I see that this 'general-and-part' thing happens again in different ways:

The 'old coats' get broken down into 'little jackets', the 'old pants' get broken down into 'little trousers'.

In the 'pockets' there are 'things'.

The 'things' break down into 'keys' and 'pennies'.

Within these, there are links through the repetitions of 'old' and 'little'. This makes 'old' with 'little' contrast. Does this accentuate the age gap? The father seems to have been older than most fathers and the children are 'little', perhaps too 'little' (too young?) to lose their father? Is that what we are told through 'old' and 'little'?

Perhaps the phrase 'your father' also has, as part of him, the children 'Dan' and 'Anne' because Dan and Anne are linked to 'father' through the word 'your'. That is, 'father' belongs to the children through 'your'. And that 'your' also links to the 'your' of 'your breakfast' and 'your medicine'. All the 'yours' make links in vertical lines from a) the speaker in the poem to the children, and b) the father to the children. This seems to tie them all together, all belonging to each other.

The future is invoked first with 'shall have' (which we hear twice). This stresses that there is a future (first with the 'things' from father's pockets: then with the repeated 'pennies' and 'keys'. Father-stuff is carried on through the poem without saying the word 'father'. These are of course basic kinship links, emphasised again.

We hear the line 'Life must go on' three times. The first one answered with 'And the dead must be forgotten', the second is answered with 'Though good men die'. The sense of these answers are of course about a departure, an ending, in relation to the idea that life must go on. And yet the repetitions and patterns before this in the poem are about what is 'taken' from the father's clothes and what 'shall' happen with them in the future. In other words, there's a contrast between what is being done (making a future) and what is being said (ending things). That's to say, the words 'And the dead must be forgotten' and 'Though good men die' are contradicted by what the speaker in the poem is actually doing, keeping the father's memory alive through what she (?) is doing with the clothes.

What does this suggest? That she is living a contradiction? Going through the motions of saying the 'right' things about forgetting while actually making sure that 'father' will be remembered through what she is doing? Yet is the sense of the poem implying that she is unaware of this contradiction?

The third time we hear the line 'Life must go on', the answer is 'I forget just why'. This is not like the other two answers. It's linked to them by virtue of being an answer (i.e. the language pattern is the same) but this time there's a contrast with the previous two answers. It's not really an answer. It's more of a kind of drifting off.

The word 'forget' is interesting. It links to 'forgotten' from before. There, forgetting was to do with the dead having to 'be forgotten', which is a homily about letting go of the memory of the dead. This 'forget' at the end of the poem is about forgetting why the dead should be forgotten! In other words, the homily is not working on the speaker. They're just empty phrases that she has repeated. This was hinted at before with the idea of the children carrying the father's 'things' into the future.

If we put rings round the word 'life' we can ask of the poem what life is made of: in other words, just as we saw generals and specifics in other parts of the poem, let's see what the specifics of 'life' are. Immediately linked to it are the facts that Anne has to eat her breakfast, and Dan has to take his medicine. The echo-link of the word 'your' (twice) as we saw before keeps the father 'alive'. But this aspect of 'life' is in the everyday necessities to stay alive – food and medicine – which directly contrast with what's happened to father, which is, of course, he died.

Other parts of the life-generality are Dan saving pennies for the bank and Anne using the keys to make a pretty noise. And before that, the making of clothes. If we put all these life-specifics together, we have the basic necessities of life: clothes (to protect us from the elements), money to live by, the keys (to the home? Or to make music? Or both?). And then the necessities I mentioned before, food and medicine.

What's happened then is that a mix of what the father has left and what the speaker is actually doing (making clothes, helping the children save and make music, have breakfast, take medicine) is the continuity of life and the means of life.

The whole poem is a knitting together of contrasts between death and life, linked together by 'secret strings'.

What I've just done here, then, is play a game or carry out a playful way to find out about the 'how' of a poem. It may help us get near to some core meaning.

Perhaps you can see some more strings.

If you think about 'stress' in phrases in English, you can see across the whole poem that there are numbers of stresses in each line. By my reckoning, no line has more than four stresses (or beats) and no line has less than two. In comparison with a lot of other writing, the overall feeling I get from this is that these lines are like short sharp bursts of speech. There is no continuity or logical carry-over from line to line. There are none of the sub-clauses that we can use in writing and speech by using 'because', 'although', 'if', 'when' or 'where' header-words. Everything is in phrases and simple sentences. These are then all linked to each other by that very fact, that they are all short sharp bursts. What does this tell us about the kind of speaking the poem is imitating – the kind of speech where we can't put together long, logical sentences with causes and conditions in them? All that she can manage are these bursts. Does it imply that she is crying or breathing in between the lines? Or heavily restraining herself, perhaps?

This secret string then runs right through the whole poem, giving it an unspoken, undescribed tone. Some poems describe their own tone: 'I am sad'. This poem doesn't. The strings I've found describe the poem's 'voice', we might say.

Another way to look at voice or tone is to ask of the lines whether they use 'figurative' language – metaphors, similes, personification. This poem is totally, or nearly totally, figurative-free. Given that we often think of poems as being particularly rich in figurative writing, then the poem as a whole sits in contrast to what a lot of other poems are like.

We might then think of words to describe this kind of writing: bald, simple, stark, factual, spare, sparse, undecorated. Is it that the speaker has no time for dwelling on what her feelings are 'like' or what's going on that is 'as if' it's something else? The weather isn't behaving in any kind of personified responsive or reflective way. This places the poem (perhaps) in a religious tradition of moderation and self-sacrifice: the Puritan tradition of avoiding excess, decoration, being fancy or self-pitying. It's the voice from the Protestant samplers that girls had to sew, saying things like 'let self-sacrifice be its own reward'. If this is true then the poem is about how a woman tries to hide her feelings but can't prevent herself from showing them in spite of herself. This belongs to a particular tradition of poetry and drama, known as 'dramatic irony', the seemingly unintentional self-revealing monologue or dialogue. In this case, it's a 'dramatic monologue' analogous to others, like Robert Browning's 'My Last Duchess', in which a male speaker unknowingly seems to reveal that he has done away with his previous wife. Is there a way in which Edna St Vincent Millay has written a reply to Browning's poem, contrasting the pompous, self-regarding male duke with a modest, caring woman? Contrast the duke, who is obsessed with how he is seen and the precious luxury items with which he has surrounded himself, with this woman who focuses on the necessities of life.

What I've just done in that last paragraph is take my secret strings out of the poem and taken them to another poem. Maybe St Vincent Millay made that string. Maybe she didn't. The point is that I've made that string, so it's part of a meaning I've made for me.

All these links tell us that we can create meanings through how we string words together beyond the level of the sentence. We make meanings to and fro through a whole passage and to outside of the passage. The jargon way of saying this is to say that we make coherence through cohesion. Things become clear and coherent through us seeing how things are cohesive, that's to say, how they are linked. Writers make cohesive writing. Readers see or feel the cohesion. If we take the strings outside of what we're reading to other readings we're exploring 'intertextuality' – the world in which strings run between books, between poems or songs, or novels, films, or any other 'text'.

If we play 'secret strings', we help ourselves make these meanings. I hope that's a fun way to get into any kind of writing.

Similes are a great way of making less-than-flattering comparisons – here are a few of my favourites:

'When I was young and working in Woolworths in Bristol, a colleague said I was as "thin as a rasher of wind".'

Linda Whitney

'Someone looking miserable had "a face as long as a yard of tripe".'

Charlotte Norman

'My grandmother, from Liverpool, used to describe people who were large as having "a head like a lodging house cat".'

Mike Smith

'As I sit here in far too many layers and with a scarf round my neck, I can almost hear my late mother saying I look like a throttled earwig.'

Liz Read

A classic from my own father, Harold Rosen. Teenage years – late nights – up late in the morning.

Dad: 'Your eyes look like two piss-holes in the snow.'

He'd also shout out to me (in bed) as he went off to work: 'Waiting till it's late enough?'

And another. My parents often produced sayings out of their Jewish background. If I tried to make a bit of an effort with what I looked like, my father would say, 'You look as sharp as a matzo ball and twice as greasy.'

Finally, when I was a teenager and doing that biceps-flexing thing, my father would say, 'My! Your muscles stand out like sparrows' kneecaps!'

'"You look like Mrs Stud." One of my grandmothers used to use it if someone was dressed to impress. It was decades later I found out it was referencing the glamorous matriarch of a travelling fairground (Studts) which travelled around South Wales.'

@RoseGee17

'As a kid, when coming home mucky, my mam would scowl at me and yell, "Look at thee! Tha's as black as t'devils nutting bags, ger in that bath!" I think a nutting bag was a sack used to store coal and/or scrounge coal off a spoil heap (hopefully one that wasn't on fire).'

@OnlyLaiking

'"You're like a flea on a rice pudding!" for someone who can't sit still. My dad (89 and from Reading) says it all the time. A friend of mine's mother used to say of someone standing around uselessly: "He/she is like a shilling dinner waiting for gravy."'

@juddmin

'"Sitting there like cheese at fourpence" from my Lancastrian great-grandmother, born 1908.'

@Collins3Collins

October

Anyone familiar with octagons and octopuses will have noticed that October is not the eighth month of our year but the tenth. As with September, November and December, the counting is awry on account of the calendar being changed. This mismatch does not seem to have bothered anyone enough early enough in the history of the naming of months for there to have been a groundswell of opinion demanding a rewrite.

The Romans thought of October as the point at which they could finish up their usual military campaigning and invading and take a rest.

Much later, October became an iconic month for some, as it marked the October Revolution of 1917 in Russia. Again, as part of the mysteries of calendar adjustments, there is a mismatch involved as the October Revolution took place in November.

Using the Venerable Bede as our guide, we could drop calling this month the numerically skewed October and go back to early speakers of Old English in Britain. 'They called the month when the winter season began Ƿintirfylliþ,' writes Bede, 'a word composed of "winter" and "full moon", because winter began on the first full moon of that month.'

Our mums and grandmothers have some of the best sayings of all. Here are a couple from my own mum.

'It's the way you're sitting.'

My mother said this a couple of times to my father when she spilled something, so it became a family alibi line for anything that went wrong. I might be out for a walk and trip up and we would say, 'It's the way you're sitting.'

'Leave him alone, he's tired.'

My mother used to say this to protect me, if she thought my brother or father were being too critical of me. They then turned it round, so that they would say it before she got a chance to say it herself. My brother might say to me in one breath, 'Look at your shoes, they're filthy, leave him alone he's tired.'

I thought it could be my epitaph on my gravestone: 'Leave him alone, he's tired.'

'"There's no pockets in a shroud." This is what my ma would say whenever she spent any significant amount of money. Which wasn't that significant, cos we didn't have any!'

@pictureladyjan

'My nan got from her nan, "You can wish in one hand and shit in the other and see what you get first!" A response to a child's pleadings, usually.'

@buteosam

'When Gran was surprised by a piece of new information, she'd say, "Lord bless us and save us, said Old Mother Davis, I never knowed bloaters was fish."'

@FranCarnell

'My mum had some great phrases she used when trying to keep some sense of order in a house with eight children. "I'll have a yard off your tail" is one that's still in use with what would be her great-grandchildren … and "I'm going to sell you and buy a rabbit"!'

Jo Harmer

'My mother taught me, "I love you lots and lots and half-a-crown". When she was small, my mother and her brother's favourite uncle would slip them half-a-crown each, much more than any other relative ever gave them, and thus it was the largest amount of money they could imagine; so they'd say to their mother, "Love you lots and lots, AND half-a-crown!" I write it in cards to my mother; might have to teach it to my kids.'

Emma-Jane Cunningham Hughes

'My English grandmother used to say someone "took the gilt off the gingerbread" to mean they diminished the joy of something. Now I find myself saying it.'

@BonkersBusway

'My wife's mother had a few – a pouting bottom lip brought the response, "you could ride to Jerusalem on that".'

@Dr_David_James

'A friend in a previous parish gave me her faux-medieval family phrase for not having to get up to do a chore when the cat is sitting on you – you claim "rights of cattage". It instantly became a core phrase in our family!'

@MirandaTHolmes

And one more from my mother, who used to say to us if our father wasn't in the room, 'Ask your father what he's doing and tell him to stop it.'

Wrong turning

My father used to tell the following joke:

'A German woman in London is standing in a queue at the butcher's shop. She turns to the person next to her and says, "I am waiting here since three hours and I have not yet become a sausage."'

I won't make any claims for the joke but the gag is based on the fact that the German word 'bekommen' does not mean 'become' but means 'to get' or 'to receive'. The bit with 'I am waiting here since three hours' was just my father throwing in the fact that anyone speaking another language often finds it difficult to translate phrases about time. To tell the truth, I think he stole the French way of saying 'I've been waiting for three hours' and put it into the mouth of someone German – but hey, I won't go there. Let's stick with 'bekommen'.

It's what translators and linguists call a 'false friend'. When we try to speak another language, we light on 'friends' – words that look or sound like a word in one language – and assume it means the same thing in another language. A famous one is 'embarazada' in Spanish, which does not mean 'embarrassed'; it means 'pregnant'. So that's the kind of false friend where an English person might say one thing but end up saying something potentially ... er ... embarrassing. There's a false friend the other way, in which you light on a word you read or hear and get it wrong when explaining it to your English friends. So, 'reins' in French are not 'reins' in English. 'Les reins' are kidneys. There are more false friends when trying to unpick the sense of a Shakespeare play: when Gloucester talks of Regan in *King Lear* as a 'naughty lady', he didn't mean that she was 'saucy' or promiscuous but that she was evil.

There's another kind of translation issue that no one calls a false friend but I could make an argument for signing these examples up to the false friends club. They are the odd or awkward mistranslations made by very learned people that then become established. Let's start with 'ego'. The story of why we say this is really rather strange. Sigmund Freud worked out a schema for our minds and the development of our minds. He wrote about the parts of this schema in German. He talked of 'das Ich', 'das Es' and 'das Über-Ich'. A plain translation of these would be 'the I', 'the It', and 'the Super-I' or 'Over-I'. 'Das Es', he thought, was the unconscious source of bodily needs, wants, emotional impulses and desires. 'Das Ich', he thought, was the means by which our minds organise these unconscious needs according to what we perceive as 'reality'. (These are very sketchy and inadequate summaries for what were and are intended to be complex processes.)

But let's get to the translations. The first of these that caught on, and has held sway ever since, translated the German as 'the ego', 'the id' and 'the superego'. These are of course Latin words – or in the case of 'superego', a concocted Latin word. So we have the odd situation in which the originator of this scheme came up with very ordinary, accessible words in his native language, but when the ideas were transferred into English, they were put into the technical language that scientists use for naming animal species and the like – Latin. I could almost make the argument that this wasn't a 'translation', it was more a re-casting, misplacing, a changing, a transformation. Another kind of false friend, perhaps.

Yet, in a way, ordinary people have had the last laugh. The term 'ego' escaped from the hands of specialists and is out there and everywhere, being used, re-used, re-applied as a word meaning something fairly different from Freud's 'Ich'. Not so with id and superego, though. They're still in the psychoanalyst's room.

Were those first translators too clever for their own good? Freud is not the only example of scholars grappling with German and coming up with false friends. Franz Kafka (who is famous enough to have been made into an eponymic adjective, Kafkaesque), produced a story that is called in German *Die Verwandlung*. A plain translation of this would be 'the transformation', particularly the kind of transformation that happens in fairy stories. Usually, when we talk about these in English we say things like '… and the sailors turned into pigs' or some such. You may notice we don't have an easy-to-use noun for what happens there: a 'turning-into' or some such. So we say, 'transformation'. Now, as it happens, the word 'Verwandlung' does have that sense of 'turning into' because the verb 'verwandeln' is how you can say 'the sailors turned into pigs'.

Die Verwandlung is the title of the book that we know in English as either *The Metamorphosis* or sometimes just *Metamorphosis*. This is a Greek word, and the one used by the Roman poet Ovid to describe a whole series of transformations in his seminal book *Metamorphoses*. It's also the word that world scientists use to describe the life cycle of insects.

Good translation of *Die Verwandlung*, we might say, because after all, doesn't the main protagonist of the story turn into an insect? Haven't we seen the pictures of a man turning into a beetle or cockroach or some kind of unnamed bug?

Ah, but did he?

In the first sentence of *Die Verwandlung*, we meet Gregor Samsa.

In German, this famous line is: 'Als Gregor Samsa eines Morgens aus unruhigen Träumen erwachte, fand er sich in seinem Bett zu einem ungeheuren Ungeziefer verwandelt.'

I'm now going to literal-translate that line word by word.

'When Gregor Samsa one morning from his uneasy dreams woke, found he in his bed into a monstrous vermin turned into.'

That's the raw literal-translation in the same order of words as the German.

Now let me give you the problem of how to turn that into English!

A very 'free' translation that would drive the specialists nuts, would be:

'One morning, Gregor Samsa woke up from his troubled dreams and found that in his bed, he had turned into some kind of monstrous vermin.'

But you know, and I know, that Gregor Samsa turned into a bug. Really? Are you sure?

The words 'ungeheuren Ungeziefer' don't say specifically that it's a bug, or an insect, or a cockroach. 'Ungeziefer' is non-specific. German people do use it to describe verminous insects like cockroaches, but it's as general as 'pest'. Later in the book, someone refers to the transformed Gregor as a 'dung beetle' but that might be a kind of colloquial joke rather than a specific name.

In other words, the way German speakers perceive that opening sentence is very different from the way English speakers perceive it.

Here's a list of translations, courtesy of Wiki, which shows us the problem:

– 'gigantic insect' (Willa and Edwin Muir, 1933)

– 'monstrous kind of vermin' (A.L. Lloyd, 1946)

– 'monstrous vermin' (Stanley Corngold, 1972; Joachim Neugroschel; 1993, Donna Freed, 1996)

– 'giant bug' (J.A. Underwood, 1981)

– 'monstrous insect' (Malcolm Pasley, 1992; Richard Stokes, 2002; Katja Pelzer, 2017)

– 'enormous bug' (Stanley Appelbaum, 1996)

– 'gargantuan pest' (M.A. Roberts, 2005)

– 'monstrous cockroach' (Michael Hofmann, 2007)

– 'monstrous verminous bug' (Ian Johnston, 2007)

– 'a vile insect, one of gigantic proportions' (Philip Lundberg, 2007)

– 'some kind of monstrous vermin' (Joyce Crick, 2009)

– 'horrible vermin' (David Wyllie, 2011)

– 'some sort of monstrous insect' (Susan Bernofsky, 2014)

– 'some kind of monstrous bedbug' (Christopher Moncrieff, 2014)

– 'large verminous insect' (John R. Williams, 2014)

– 'a kind of giant bug' (William Aaltonen, 2023)

Take your pick!

Kafka himself was very keen for there not to be an illustration of an insect on the cover of the book. I can think of several reasons for this:

Kafka didn't think that Samsa had turned into an insect but had turned into something else. (Some people say that's doubtful because he and his friends did refer to the story as the 'Wanzensache' – literally the 'bug-thing' or, as we might say, 'your bug piece'.)

Kafka thought that Samsa had turned into an insect but didn't want people to think precisely that in the opening sentence. That's because the point of view, at this exact point in the story, is what Samsa feels. He feels as if he's turned into some kind of monstrous verminous thing. Perhaps at that point neither he nor we know what kind of a monstrous verminous thing.

Kafka didn't create a story about someone actually turning into a bug or any kind of vermin. The story is about how someone sees himself, and then, as a result of that perception of himself, how others see him. In other words, it might be a bug-piece, it might be about bugs and vermin, but not because he's actually turned into one. This makes the book about perception, self-image, how self-image affects others, how the way in which others perceive our self-image then affects us and on and on and on, in a hall of mirrors. This kind of 'reflexivity' has a name: 'dialectics', and German philosophy has often been very interested in dialectics. Perhaps that opening sentence, one of the most famous in all of literature, grasped the essence of dialectics.

But hang on, why would someone wake up out of troubled dreams and think that he is a gigantic piece of horrible vermin? Aha, and that leads scholars down the biographical route of what it was like being Kafka, in Prague, at that time, with the kinds of parents he had, being despised for being Jewish, or despised by his father for being himself …

Meanwhile, pity the poor translator, eh?

One other thing: that phrase 'ungeheuren Ungeziefer'. If you don't know how to say it, just go online and find an audio of it. It's beautiful! The two words both begin with the same two syllables and the next syllable is stressed. Try saying 'disgustingly disgusted' or (absurdly) 'undecided undercarriage' and you get a sense of the sound of it. The two words echo each other, or bounce off each other. They'd be a gift to drummers and jazz musicians. In fact, when I'm feeling shitty (excuse the language, but I'm trying to stick with the theme of disgust), I whisper to myself, 'Ungeheuren Ungeziefer, ungeheuren Ungeziefer, ungeheuren Ungeziefer.'

Some people say that Kafka is depressing and offers us no way out. I think this misses the point. By describing hell, I take it that we should do things to avoid the hells he describes. I uplift myself by finding it amusing that I'm using the very phrase that expresses Gregor Samsa's (and Kafka's?) sense of being the kind of thing which he thinks, in the opening sentence, people around him would find disgusting.

A sheynem dank, Franz.

(Thanks very much, Franz. [Yiddish])

Now to East Anglia:

'"On the huh": Norfolk saying for lopsided. "That picture is on the huh."'

@kate_mate_68

'I have remembered one from my Suffolk nan. Her invariable "grace" before meals was: "What we're about to receive is nothing to do with them in the village"!'

@Miller_Klein

'Mum has a mid-Essex dialect and says things like "peggles" for cowslips; "post lauders" for postal order; "I've got a bone in me leg" for pain; "queer" means ill; "tater" for potato; "tiddy" for tiny; "grizzling" for crying; "I'll learn him to do that" for teach; and "unhonest".'

@Ettedo9

'My gran (from Essex) had lots of odd expressions. Two that spring to mind are "You'll strain your haikey flukus" if you were exerting yourself, and "You'd break old inky if he came to town" when I'd trash my toys. I've never seen or heard these anywhere else. Phonetically it would have been high-key flookus.'

@bigmave

'Keep you a-troshin'' (literally means 'carry on threshing' but usually for saying goodbye, keep going!).

'To mardle' means 'to gossip'.

(This reminds me that my father wrote in his memoir that he and his friends used to sit on the steps and 'have a muttel' – that is, have a chat. I've yet to find anyone who can speak Yiddish or German who recognises the word!)

Tadpoles are a rich source for variation. In Norfolk, they're pollywiggles.

Again in Norfolk, a ladybird can be a bushy barn-a-bee.

If you're in Norfolk, you might call a person you're friendly with 'bor', whereas in other parts of Britain or the world you might say 'mate', 'matey', 'love', 'pal', 'bach', 'la', 'hen', 'duck', 'son', 'sunny jim', 'gal', 'feller', 'bruv', 'spa', 'boyo', 'boychik' … add your own!

'On the drag' in Suffolk means 'running late'.

Up in the World
If ever I open up a conversation on Twitter/X about language, I can be sure that some people will join in in order to rage at a usage they detest. So, people rage about 'so'. 'Why is everyone using "so"?' they say. 'Everything begins with "so", nowadays.' I don't have an answer to this or hardly any of the other complaints. Why do people opt for new usages for old

words? In some way or another, these new ways of speaking must feel as if the new usages can do a good job, given present circumstances. This way of using 'so' is both a summing-up kind of word and also what is called a 'discourse-marker'. That's to say, it marks a point in a conversation or piece of writing, where the speaker/writer signals something to do with that bit of language itself. This means 'so' can announce that we've reached a break in what we're saying or writing, or a 'therefore', or a 'what's going to come next is what I reckon is going on', or even just 'I'm taking a moment to reflect, stick with me here'.

Why would we need this more now than we did 30 years ago? Here are some speculations: is it something to do with the rapidity of how we share information, combined with the sheer amount of information? Is 'so' doing the job of pulling things together, taking a pause, signalling in a heavily congested information-swapping society that the speaker needs a tiny break but please don't interrupt while I'm taking a breather?

Another bugbear is the way we can turn nouns into verbs. A particularly loathed one is 'medalled'. Athletes talk about 'medalling', and how glad they are that they 'medalled'. When people object to a usage like this, they say things like: 'But "medal" is a noun, not a verb!' Sad to say, but this is a misunderstanding of how we make language work. Any word that I put on the page, isolated from other words, is in itself not a noun, or a verb, or an adjective or anything else. It only becomes a noun, verb, adjective or any of the other kinds of word when it's in phrases, sentences and passages of speech and writing. Dictionaries are partly to blame for this, because if you look up 'medal', it has been saying '(n)' (for noun) next to it for centuries. That's because that is mostly how it's been used. The point is that it may be 'mostly' or even 'always up until now' – but it isn't inevitable. If someone wants to 'verb' the word 'medal', they can. At this point, dictionaries jump to it (some have already), and write a new line: 'Medal (v)' for verb.

Even so, there's a mistaken assumption that all this verbing is new. Nothing could be further from the truth. Take a word like 'deal'. It's very much both a (n) and a (v): 'I got a good deal' and 'Deal the cards, Mum'. I've been back through the *Oxford English Dictionary* and it's clear that people have been saying either or both for hundreds of years. I've never heard anyone say that they're uncomfortable with either, either – if you get me!

If you want some nice examples of how adaptable we are with our words, then try my favourites: the words we say are prepositions. Take 'up'. We call it a preposition because that's what words like 'up' are called, when they're in phrases like this: 'Up the Junction', 'up the wall'. Look more closely and there's another kind of 'up' when we make what are called 'phrasal verbs'. With 'up' linked to a verb, we can give direction to the action of a verb: 'Big up that guy over there, he's not very confident'. (Notice 'big', which is mostly an adjective, being made into a verb there!) The 'up' linked to 'big' raises 'that guy', lifts him up. We can't extract 'up that guy' from 'big up that guy' in the way that we can extract 'up the wall' from a sentence like 'I saw a spider crawling up the wall'.

Why not? Because the 'unit' is 'big up' not 'up that guy'.

Similarly, we can say 'I threw up' to mean 'I vomited', and that's different from 'I threw the ball up into the air'. 'I threw up this morning's breakfast' breaks into 'I threw up' and 'this morning's breakfast', but the other sentence breaks into 'I threw the ball' and 'up into the air'.

Now here's a funny thing: when we turn 'this morning's breakfast' into 'it' (a 'pronoun'), we put it in a different place in the sentence: 'I threw it up', same as the construction for the ball, 'I threw it up into the air'. The 'it' goes in between 'threw' and 'up'. Why? I dunno.

And yet, mysteriously, there are occasions when that 'it' can be like the noun and stay after the 'up'. Let's try this: 'I don't want to go up the mountain today.' 'Oh come on, Michael, you really should go up it today, it's going to rain tomorrow.'

Hah! 'Go up it' not 'go it up'.

If you would like to get your head round classifications and categories, you can go online and visit 'separable' and 'non-separable' phrasal verbs. You can even look at 'transitive' and 'non-transitive' phrasal verbs and then have some fun seeing whether grammarians can sort out whether to call these different 'ups' prepositions, adverbs or, my fave, what they call 'particles'. And after you've had a good long bath in these, see if you can figure out any kind of explanation as to why we can say 'go up it' and not 'go it up' but we say 'throw it up' and not 'throw up it'. When I say 'explanation', I don't mean by way of a rule or even a pattern. I mean, how it is that this is what we have created. Is there some purpose or reason for it?

More fun now with 'up' and these functions, as they're called. How about this: I was standing in a gym in Australia and a woman coach said to the guy next to me, 'Time to up the reps, Pete.' Love it! 'Up' as a verb. ('Reps' are repetitions of exercises.) Ever since, it's become one of my slogans. If I do five squats while I'm microwaving my soup, I say to myself, 'Time to up the reps, Pete.'

Earlier, I talked of 'up' as a preposition in a phrase. But can you have 'up' as a dangling preposition on its own with nothing after it? I went to Oxford University, which rejoices in many bits of in-group jargon (including and excluding at the same time). One college is not known by its name. It's just called 'House'. Broad Street is not called Broad Street, it's 'The Broad'. The Bodleian Library is called 'The Bod' or, back in the day, 'Bodley'. The Eagle and Child pub is called 'the Bird and Baby' and on and on and on. But what does one person say to another if they think that they've both been to Oxford? They say, 'Were you up?' It's almost a secret sign, like a red carnation, or a rolled umbrella held in the left hand. It's code for saying that we're part of the same club or network, aren't we?

My brother and I were both 'up' and we exist in an ambivalent space in which we both know that we owe an enormous lot to Oxford University, while not being totally comfortable with the way in which we've been admitted into an elite. (A matter that is far, far, far from being the most important discomfort in the world, I hastily admit.)

So my brother and I created a category which we speak of or write as 'Upp'. Upp is a state of mind, or a way of talking, or a way in which a TV interview has been conducted, or the way in which someone has written up their life. If we hear some kind of chumminess going on between an interviewer or politician, say, one or other of us will shout, 'Upp'. We're guessing or assuming that both interviewer and interviewee are Upp or are being Upp. That way it's an adjective. We both know that whether we like it or not, we're Upp too. We can spot others being Upp because we were up. Others might say, we're up ourselves, but that's another matter.

Any more 'up'? When we speak English we can add bits to words, to change meanings and functions. One way is to put bits on the front (prefixes) and bits on the end (suffixes and endings).

So we might start with 'happy'. To make it mean something else, we can say 'unhappy'. To give it a different function, we can say 'happiness'. So here they are in sentences: 'Happy days are here again (adjective); 'I thought he was an unhappy little boy' (change of meaning, staying as an adjective); and 'Happiness can creep up on you like a cat looking to be stroked' (change of function – it's now a noun).

What can we do with 'up'? Well, we can do anything with it. There are no language police or gods to tell us we can't. The poet Gerard Manley Hopkins proves that (see page 190) and in many of his poems we see him creating new meanings and new functions.

Someone (possibly the author of a cricket article in the *Morning Star* newspaper of 1862 – not to be confused with the better-known Communist paper from the twentieth century), used the word 'uppish', which had, since the seventeenth century, mostly been a word about class, to refer to what happens to a ball after a batsman hits it: 'Hayward sends a long uppish hit' (source: *OED*).

If a ball goes up in the air, there's a possibility that some-one will catch it, and the batsman will be 'out' (another example of adapting what was usually a preposition to make it an adjective). A ball can be on the ground, very much up in the air, or it can be a little bit up in the air. The *Morning Star* journalist (if it was he) adapted a usage in order to describe 'a bit up in the air'. I've even heard 'uppishly' too (adverb).

But on this journey into our ingenuity with the English language, we're not done with 'up' yet. I mentioned prefixes and suffixes. We can get 'up' to do a great job here too. There's been an 'uptick' in interest in this matter but others think it's a bit of a 'screwup'. With 'screwup' we're back with phrasal verbs. When we make nouns or adjectives out of phrasal verbs, we have to decide where to put the particle. The 'outgoing' chairperson, the 'upshot' of the meeting, a 'standout' example, 'incoming' wind, atomic 'fallout', 'check-out', 'input', 'output', 'throughput' …

That gives us a space to make up absurd and quaint versions ourselves:

It was a very 'peteredout' session, I thought.

The cracks were showing so he went for 'overpapering' rather than dealing with it.

Worrying sign: a big 'uprun' in his bills.

If you make bracelets or necklaces with coloured beads, you'll know that you can make and change sequences in order to produce different looks. This is what we do with English. In fact, as an analogy, this works pretty well to describe what we do when we make words with prefixes and suffixes; when we put 'endings' on words to make plurals or verb forms; and when we make phrases, clauses, sentences and whole passages of conversation, speaking and writing. We string together parts of words and whole words. They are 'togetherstrung'.

(By the way, on some plurals, we'll have to change the bead itself. That's because we don't use the usual 's', and 'es', or even 'knife-knives' or the unusual 'r + en' in 'children'. What we do is say 'foot-feet', 'tooth-teeth' and 'woman-women'. No matter, the beads can do the job.)

Another Rosen classic. There's a famous French comic song about a servant supposed to be guarding the chateau but everything goes wrong. When the marquise calls, he assures her it's all fine: 'Tout va très bien, Madame la Marquise.' My parents sang it whenever things were going wrong.

'We local kids used to make bows and arrows. The arrows were from bamboo in the park. Every year one or other set of parents would tell us about the kid who lost an eye doing this. None of us ever met that kid. "You'll have someone's eye out with that."'

@drpaulitious

'"There's no back door on the ocean!" Meaning there's no way out of a situation, it has to be faced. (From an aunt, years ago, on learning that an unmarried daughter was pregnant.) I've often used it but not for the same reason! It always raises a quizzical look and a smile.'

@emzialzi

'If I overindulged on sweets, my great-aunt used to say, "You'll get worms." Naturally, I always thought she was referring to earthworms, so I was confused more than concerned.'

@RichardLafette

'My grandmother, a dressmaker, used the term "obble-gobble stitch and bunch work" for any piece of poorly executed sewing. Strangely, you can picture it exactly from that description!'

@frdragonspouse

'My grandmother (from Bassenthwaite) used to say, of a merrily carefree person, "They were laughin' cakes a-blackin'." My mother carried it on, and I recently caught myself saying it.'

@toooldforit

What does the phrase book say?

In one of my Yiddish classes we had to learn how to say, 'Your fruit is worse than my fruit.'

As we said it, I tried to think of a situation in which I would need to say this. I guess it could come in handy if I was a greengrocer who hadn't been to the wholesaler to pick up fresh supplies talking to another greengrocer who hadn't been to the wholesaler to pick up fresh supplies. Quite niche, then. I posted it up on Twitter/X and some others came back:

Ruth Hunter said, 'I learned Russian in Russia, and my first sentence was, "I'm not a duck, I'm a black swan".'

Pie Corbett wrote: 'Fifty years ago, working with Polish students, the manual directed us to learn the English for "my parachute has not opened".'

This made me think that phrasebook writers could write special editions titled *Famous Last Words*.

Pie added: 'My other favourite from the manual was, "Where can I empty the contents of my chemical toilet?"' He didn't say what the correct answer was.

It seems that Duolingo, the online language-learning site, has cottoned on to this and they're deliberately putting out jokey lines for people to translate or say in the language they are learning.

Lorna posted: 'I'm learning Italian on Duolingo and recently had to translate this: "My cat Leonardo has a driver's licence but he can't drive your car anyway." Essential learning for beginners,' she adds.

Fiona Thompson wrote: 'My favourite so far is: "Where are my spider's clothes?" Duolingo Greek at its finest.'

Sam Pope wrote, 'When trying to learn Russian with Duolingo, I had to say, "The horse is in the taxi" and "You are not my father".'

A recent article in *The Economist*, in an article called 'Phrasebooks are dying out. It is the end of a revealing literary genre' (27 October 2022), revealed a few old classics.

It cites the writer Eric Newby who set out to walk the Hindu Kush in 1956. He carried a phrase book published in Calcutta in 1902, *Notes on the Bashgali Language*. From this he learned how to say, 'I saw a corpse in a field this morning', 'I have nine fingers; you have ten' and 'How long have you had a goitre?'

The article goes on:

> The 1900 English-Welsh phrasebook *For the use of Travellers and Students* offers 'Have you any apples?' and 'Where is the butter market?' before adding the more unexpected: 'They have cut off his arm.' [...]
>
> J.B. Leek's 1928 *English-Italian Conversation Handbook* [has] a section on hair care ('Shave my mustachio / Kindly twist up my mustachio / A little pomade on my mustachio'). [...]
>
> A 1903 medical phrasebook for Luganda, a Bantu language, offers the unexplained but authoritative: 'Keep everything you vomit.' [...]

The 1909 *Manual of Palestinian Arabic* explains that its sample sentences 'will, it is hoped, be useful to the traveller in his hotel' and 'may conceivably be of use in daily life'. The word 'conceivably' is working very hard in that sentence. The book's phrases include: 'We reached the precipice and saw him fall down'. [...]

When Elisabeth Kendall, the mistress of Girton College, Cambridge, studied Arabic at Oxford University in the early 1990s, she did so using grammar books that dated back to 1859. '"The cow's tongue is long" was a typical phrase,' she said.

Phrase books are indeed a genre of their own.

Are they dying out? Has the internet pushed them over the 'precipice' and are we seeing them 'fall down'?

'In my family, who spent much of their time in Manchester, Chester and rural Wales, over many decades, my mother and grandparents used the phrase, "I don't boil my cabbages twice" if you misheard or asked them to repeat a comment. Instead of repeating, they might say, "I don't boil my cabbages twice!"'

Linden Linn

'If we weren't feeling well, my mother would ask, "Have you been?" If not then it was prunes, which were called "black-coated workers", for obvious reasons.'

@Stitchandsow

'If we were feeling a bit under the weather, Mum would tell us to stick our tongue out and, having assessed the state of it, she'd say, "You want some opening medicine." It wasn't until many years later I realised "opening medicine" was syrup of figs.'

@CarolCarman

I recognise yesterday's phrases, because my own mum had intimate knowledge of food that was 'loosening' and food that was 'binding'. Loosening was generally good and necessary – prunes, beetroot and onion in vinegar, raisins. Binding was bad unless you had the squits – too many eggs, and arrowroot powder in the larder.

November

'Novem' means 'nine' in Latin, and November was the ninth month in early Roman times. The Roman calendar seems stuffed full of what they called 'Plebeian Games'. There's a hint that this means they were popular festivals going back before the time of the establishment of Rome itself. Perhaps the Roman rulers worked to the rule of thumb that it was better from their point of view to incorporate and accept ancient festivals rather than to suppress them.

Thomas Hood (1799–1845) didn't think November was much use. He wrote:

> No sun—no moon!
>   No morn—no noon—
> No dawn—
>   No sky—no earthly view—
>   No distance looking blue—
> No road—no street—no 't'other side the way'—
>   No end to any Row—
>   No indications where the Crescents go—
>   No top to any steeple—
> No recognitions of familiar people—
>   No courtesies for showing 'em—
>   No knowing 'em!
> No travelling at all—no locomotion,
> No inkling of the way—no notion—
>   'No go'—by land or ocean—
>   No mail—no post—
>   No news from any foreign coast—
> No park—no ring—no afternoon gentility—
>   No company—no nobility—

No warmth, no cheerfulness, no healthful ease,
  No comfortable feel in any member—
No shade, no shine, no butterflies, no bees,
No fruits, no flowers, no leaves, no birds,
  November!

In Old English, November was Blōtmōnaþ. It's tempting to translate this as 'Blood Month' (and some do) but 'Blōt' rather means 'sacrifice' and 'worship'. The Venerable Bede notes: 'This month is called Novembris in Latin, and in our language the month of sacrifice, because our forefathers, when they were heathens, always sacrificed in this month, that is, that they took and devoted to their idols the cattle which they wished to offer.'

So, yes, there was a lot of blood, as there is if you slaughter cattle and offer them up to the gods, but strictly speaking not 'Blood Month'.

'My mother from Barnsley would say, when someone was surprised, that their eyes "stuck out like chapel hat-pegs". I loved that.'

Vicky Ireland

'"Dim as a Toc H lamp", meaning dim-witted. I grew up in Loughton where there was a Toc H house/church and it was a common phrase used in the area.' (Toc H is a Christian association for social service.)

@kashmir58

'My mam, from South Shields, had sayings for when you were stood there doing nothing like "Stood there like one of Lipton's".'

Harry Spooner

'"Silly as a sack-load of wind" – a favourite of my dad's and still used by his kids and grandchildren.'

@annpugh

If, like me, you're from 'the south' we talk about a huge area in the north of England as 'the North East'. When I go there (which I often have), I'm soon reminded that it's not one region but several, each with distinct ways of talking. That should be obvious just by looking at the geography of big cities like Newcastle and Sunderland, the country areas of Northumberland and County Durham, coastal villages and towns and much else.

People sent in expressions from all over the area:

'A favourite Tyneside expression: "worky ticket". Someone who's being mischievous and stirring up trouble. Some say it goes back to the days when criminals would be shipped off to faraway places. A worky ticket would be working their way towards earning their ticket home!'

@CGrahamPoetUK

'"Marra" refers to friends/family where I was from in the North East. One of my favourite phrases growing up, that I like to confuse people with today, is "cuddy wifter", aka left-handed.'

@ScoutMocking

'"Spelk" – I didn't realise until I moved away from the North East that this word, meaning a small splinter, isn't used outside the region. It was used all the time growing up. "Have you got a spelk in your finger?"'

@epidemic27

'"Cowp ya creels" (coastal Northumberland/North Shields) – means to trip over something and fall. From my grandad.'

@PhilipBagLowe

'A "fitchy-fatch" was a strange creature that lurked in holes and corners and its existence explained the unexplained. So a mysterious hole was made by/contained fitchy-fatches, missing items were stolen by them, etc. From my dad/granda, County Durham.'

@aunty_cis

Why are we amused and delighted by the way our babies, toddlers and children speak? Some of it is because they seem to be coining new words and that can seem very clever. Other times it's because there's something mysterious about how their brains work: they hear a word (many times perhaps) but when they come to say it, it comes out differently. It's as if the wiring between hearing and speaking hasn't quite been put in yet. And then, if we as adults are tickled by these, we often like to hang on to them, as a memory of the childhoods of our now grown-up children.

'Copterdodo: my daughter's way of saying helicopter.'

@MakingSendse

'When I created unidentifiable things as a child – a drawing, or a Lego or plasticine sculpture, for example – my parents would call it a "bloot".'

@FritzdorfSport

'My friend's small nephew called people on motorbikes "motorbikalists". This makes so much more sense linguistically. We now say bikeler and bikalist for people on pushbikes and struggle to remember the real words.'

Anna Park

A bit of my own Rosen kidspeak. My word for chocolate when I was very young was 'gub-gub'. That stayed in the family for years with everyone calling chocolate 'gub-gub'.

'Gook gook – apparently my dad couldn't say chicken when he was little. It's stuck and now my children say it. Although Dad is gone, it's like a little bit of him every time I hear it.'

@SianCafferkey

'Grandma was at our house heating up milk for my toddler son and asked him if I usually put it in the microwave. He answered very firmly, "That's not your crowave, that's our crowave." Forever known as an "ourcrowave" now. Ours is called the milkowave, thanks to our youngest, who'd mainly seen it used to warm up milk at bedtime. Kid is nearly 15 now but I still call it that.'

@lynch_ek

'Poppygarga: my daughter's way of saying grandad.'

@MakingSendse

My late son, when he was a toddler, started talking about the 'smeenge'. We had no idea what he was talking about. We tried saying it back to him but the point about this mismatch between input and output is that the youngsters don't hear the word as the way they pronounce it. In the end, we figured it was 'machine'. And that could be a washing machine or a machine he was making with Lego. I still use it. Lovely memory to have of him.

One of my children talked of biscuits as 'prets'. Why? Did she hear the last part of 'biscuits' as 'prets'? It became easy to call them that from then on.

Some English words seem to be universally hard for very young children to say. 'Helicopters' are often 'helicockters', 'spaghetti' is often 'pasketti', and 'hippopotamus' (as with one of my children) is 'hippen-hopanus'. It seemed harder to say than the original!

One of my children got very cross with me. We were wrestling and I was winning. He was about four. I really should have eradicated the competitive spirit in myself. Anyway, he leaped up. He was very angry and he stood over me and clearly he wanted to swear. But no swear word came to mind. So he had to invent one. He stood there, pointing at me, and finally came out with, 'You … you … you bear-poo!'

That's a very clever lad, I thought. He's thought of something horrible and something big and fierce, and matched the two together to coin a brand-new word.

The elephant in the syndrome

Here's a list of ways in which we can describe ourselves and our behaviour, whether as individuals, individuals in groups or individuals in society:

1) Syndromes, laws, principles, paradoxes, social theories, fallacies, complexes, conditions, effects, traits, characteristics, idioms to represent behaviours, linguistic patterns and literary terms ...

When you read that list, what examples did you think of? Any of these?

2) Occam's razor, Schroedinger's cat, Parkinson's law, the Peter principle, whataboutery, gaslighting, sealioning, elephant in the room, confirmation bias, cognitive bias, cognitive dissonance, Stockholm syndrome, passive-aggressive, in denial, hegemony, cultural capital, critical race theory, horseshoe theory, sense of entitlement, performative behaviour, emotional intelligence, Dunning-Kruger effect.

3) Or how about some older ones: hubris, catharsis, pathetic fallacy, dramatic irony, deus ex machina, esprit d'escalier, post hoc ergo propter hoc, harmony, bile, chivalry, divine right, fate, fortune, advancement ...?

I am putting these lists in front of you because I have a puzzle. The first list (syndromes, etc.) was my attempt to find names for a range of terms we use in order to put into categories the ways we understand each other. I've done this because I have a sense that we are creating and using more and more of these kinds of terms. And I would add that this change involves some kind of shift in language and thought. In short, we have 'social-psychologised' our behaviour. Social psychology is the study of how we think and behave when we're in groups or in society as a whole. Central to this is how we use language to describe our thoughts and behaviour. If we've 'social-psychologised' ourselves (my theory!) then what I'm saying is that we name and categorise the way we think, talk, write and behave when we're in groups more than we used to.

As with any science or pseudo-science, there are a) the phenomena (things, stuff, processes) and b) the terms to describe the phenomena. However, the terms that we come up with will affect how (or even whether) we see the phenomena. Example: if I say that the heart is the seat of our emotions, that encourages me to see the heart differently from my saying that the heart houses two pumps. I 'see' the heart in different ways.

This way, the terms (the way we talk about the phenomena) become phenomena in themselves. We can even give this a name: 'reflexivity'.

Humans have been trying to come up with language (terms) to describe phenomena for centuries, but the way we do this changes over the years. In other words, reflexivity changes.

This means that the things we notice change, old terms die out, our ways of noticing change. Example: it's not easy to get into the minds of Elizabethans but we have help from Shakespeare and others. In a play, we see that Hamlet sees (or imagines) an apparition of his father. This ghost tells him that Hamlet's uncle, the ghost's brother, killed him and so what Hamlet has to do is revenge that murder. Hamlet vows to do this.

A couple of problems here: would Elizabethan audiences have thought to themselves, 'Yes, do what the ghost tells you, Hamlet'? Or would they have thought, 'Don't do it, Hamlet, listening to ghosts will end badly'? Possibly either or both? I'm guessing that there weren't any people thinking, 'Now that's an interesting way to represent the suspicions and conflicts in Hamlet's mind arising out of the fact that he loves his mother and is jealous of his uncle marrying her. So what he's doing is idealising his father (who he was also jealous of) when really it's his own forbidden desire for his mother that he's struggling with. It's the Oedipus complex being played out here.'

In other words, I'm asking, have our minds changed since Elizabethan times? And if so, our ways of representing that change would be the new language that we've developed for describing our minds and behaviours.

In antagonistic situations in the workplace, in meetings, in relationships and on social media, people have learned how to make the 'field' of these terms part of the battle between ourselves. We say to each other, 'You're in denial', 'That's whataboutery', 'This firm is working on the Peter principle', 'You're gaslighting me', 'The elephant in the room is …', etc.

Question: are these new terms helping us or are we making things even more complicated for ourselves? Do new terms open our eyes for us, liberate us from being trapped in some invisible patterns of behaviour that are controlling us? Is it working like this: I might think I'm doing my job in my firm or my organisation but I can't figure out why the organisation itself is doing badly. Then one day someone tells me about the Peter principle: 'everyone is promoted to their level of incompetence'. (It's a nice reversal of what people might say is the pattern in the workplace, i.e. that competent people get promoted and hand their expertise on to the new folks.)

In my little scenario here, this Peter principle (new to me in my workplace) becomes a sudden eye-opener for me. It becomes a new prism through which I start to see how things are going wrong in my organisation.

Theory: can I say that as the world becomes more complicated, more dense with information and more dense with people, I need more and more terms (language) to help me understand what's going on?

I can see a problem with this: I could study these terms for so long, that I never get round to doing anything about the things that the terms describe (joke).

But I care about you, dear reader. I want this book to delight and enlighten you. So I'm going to give you a list of some of these terms and I want you to see if you can explain or define them. If you score more than 50 per cent this will show that you are proficient, but as with a lot of tests and exams, I can't tell you what you are now proficient in. Better still, make it a party game: see who scores the highest and then punish or shame this winner for being so knowledgeable about other people's failings. They need to take a look at themselves. As my mother would have said to them: 'Is it nice? Is it necessary?' (By the way, that was one of her jokes.)

I've mentioned some of these syndromes already. The game can be made more complicated by contestants naming effects, laws and syndromes not mentioned in the list. Wikipedia is helpful for lists of paradoxes, syndromes, effects, traits, complexes, etc.

There's scope here too for bluffing. Contestants can invent syndromes and pass them off as real. Or they might be real. If the other contestants believe a false syndrome, you score. If they spot that it's false, they score. Extra points for making people laugh – whether it's true or not. Some of the following are literary tropes rather than pure behavioural types.

Peter principle	KISS principle
Schroedinger's cat	Russell's teapot
Parkinson's law	Pathetic fallacy
Whataboutery	Eucatastrophe
Gaslighting	In media res
Dunning-Kruger effect	Predestination paradox
Founder's syndrome	Fatal flaw
Negative selection	Hubris
Selective outrage	Deus ex machina
Putt's law	McGuffin
Pareto principle	Shoulder angel
Lateral thinking	Storge
Thinking outside the box	Agape
Pushing the envelope	Harm avoidance
Institutional racism (sexism, etc.)	Authority bias
	Big lie
Elephant in the room	Cognitive distortion
Big fish, little pond	Confabulation
Cognitive dissonance	Creeping normality
PLUs (people like us)	DARVO
Cognitive bias	Martha Mitchell effect
Hanlon's razor	Stockholm syndrome
Impostor syndrome	Zersetzung
Optimism bias	Ichschmerz
Occam's razor	Weltschmerz
Chekov's gun	Colonial gaze
Cunningham's law	Atlas personality
Hickham's dictum	Codependence
Hitchens' razor	Blame the victim

Horseshoe theory

Projection

Displacement

Condensation

Labelling theory

Just-world fallacy

Emotional intelligence

Coping strategies

Dyscopia

Hope theory

Passive-aggressive

Dark triad

Gaming the system

Let the Wookiee win

Oneupmanship

Malicious compliance

Relational aggression

Romance fraud

Mobbing

Online disinhibition effect

Web mining

Acton's dictum

Clarke's three laws

Hick's law

Isaac Bonewits's law of
  magic

Littlewood's law

Rosenthal effect

Teeter's law

Abilene paradox

Hedgehog's dilemma

Region-beta paradox

Stapp's ironic paradox

Birthday number effect

Coolidge effect

Gell-Mann amnesia effect

Hawthorne effect

Lake Wobegon effect

Ovsiankina effect

Rashomon effect

Ringelmann effect

Tinkerbell effect

Tocqueville paradox

A Veblen good

Woozle effect

Saviour complex

Cassandra complex

Cinderella complex

Icarus complex

Jonah complex

Phaeton complex

Student syndrome

Let me slot in one of my own: Prince Hal syndrome – deliberate non-remembering.

In the plays, *Henry IV Parts I and II*, Prince Hal hangs out with some lowlifes, the most memorable of whom is Falstaff. This is in itself scandalous. Hal's father (Henry IV) is not happy about it. Then Henry IV dies, so Hal becomes king – Henry V. Falstaff thinks that the old relationship will continue but when he presents himself to Hal, Hal says, 'I know thee not, old man.'

It's a fascinating moment of what we might call today 'performative non-remembering'. That's to say, for the knock-about, boozy Hal to transform himself into the calculating monarch, he has to show ('performative') that he doesn't 'know' Falstaff and that way of life. It's a form of censorship through staged silence.

So in among all these other syndromes, principles, effects, traits, tropes and 'razors', I'm going to suggest Prince Hal syndrome. This is any event, story, occasion that grabs the news, preoccupies people, is apparently important but then when the situation changes, it's no longer news, it's not important. In other words, there is 'performative non-remembering'.

I'm sure you can think of examples from politics, culture, your own personal lives. It happened to me (that's to say the performative non-remembering), so I needed a name for it.

Isn't this one way in which language works? We spot a 'semantic gap' (something that exists and has meaning, but we don't have words for it), and so we come up with an expression.

We end the month with some great Scottish phrases to celebrate St Andrew's Day.

St Andrew is one of the apostles, and it's not known exactly why or how he became the patron saint of Scotland. Two legends explain the matter differently: one is that he came to Scotland and built a church in Fife at what is now St Andrews. The other is that some relics of St Andrew were brought to Fife.

When it comes to language, we should rightly speak of several languages and dialects past and present, some of which are Scots Gaelic, Lowland Scots, Broad Scots, Lallans and Doric. It is a gloriously rich and complex story of settlements, wars, conquests and resistance that scholars have pored over for hundreds of years.

We received some tiny hints of this in our contributions.

'I've inherited mony Scots words and phrases fae ma mum and dad who were Scots speakers fae Midlothian/ East Lothian. "Thon's a souster" = that's big, "ye donnart-eidjit" = silly idiot, "wrocht tae daith" = hattered/exhausted fae rushing about, are just some.'

@LearningHoolet

'When we were being greedy – just wanting stuff, especially if someone else had it – my Glaswegian dad, Alec Aitken, would say to us, "You ne'er saw green cheese but your een dain't dance." It refers to jealousy. When I was small, I just thought it referred to food greed.

My mother's family were from the west coast of Scotland. My favourites are "Awa' an' bile yer heid", and the one before the one for the road: "A wee clochan dichter".'

Chris Wallis

'"Here's tae us, wha's like us, gey few and they're a' deid."
Translation: Here's to us and those like us, there's very few
[like us] and most of them are dead.'

@TheRobinsClass

The Oxford Reference online says:

> Here's tae us; wha's like us? / Gey few, and they're a' deid.
> Anonymous: Scottish toast, probably of 19th-century
> origin; the first line appears in T.W.H. Crosland *The
> Unspeakable Scot* (1902), and various versions of the
> second line are current.

'My father's: "Tak awa Aeberdeen an twal mal roon an fit
hae ye?" (Take away Aberdeen and 12 miles around and what
have you?) In the Aberdeen dialect, 'wh' is pronounced 'f': fit
(what), foo (how), fit wye (why – what way), etc.'

@angusdawalker

'Mind your feet on the lobby gas ... my mum (Fife) said it
when we were young. It was usually a warning that we were
on the edge of getting into trouble!'

@MaryKDoherty

'Only need the distance of a few miles for the words to change up that way. Like in Peterhead you would call an Aberdeen roll a buttery or even a cookie but in Aberdeen they're a rowie.'

@KerryKe98646929

'Raised by a Scottish nanny who talked of "switching" eggs for "whisking" eggs. Posh me at posh school rebuked by cookery teacher for using the wrong word.'

@shirlsFranklin

'My Glaswegian grandmother used to say, "Aw your arse is in parsley", meaning "you're speaking nonsense".'

Anna Portch

'A couple from growing up in Galloway, south-west Scotland. Growing up my mum and dad told me we lived in "the erse end of Scotland". The bottom! My favourite word was "foonert". Every morning in winter they would say "I'm fair foonert in here, get the fire on." Foonert is a little-used Scots word for "cold through to the bone".'

Gordon Henry

Thanks to Judith Lowans Thurley for some fantastic examples:

My mum and dad had lots of Ulster-Scots.

- 'Ach, yer heid's out the winda' or 'yer bum's a plum' is 'you're talking nonsense'.

- 'A quare sprochlin' match', is struggling to do something awkward like get out of e.g. a low chair or a car, though a lot of people spell and pronounce it sprachlin.

- 'Pochlin'' or 'futherin' (footerin') about' is pottering about and achieving not very much.

- 'Thon' means that, and we use it a lot.

- My grandparents and aunts and uncles on my dad's side would say 'dooinz' for any ould thing they'd forgotten the name of or couldn't be bothered naming: 'Pass us the dooinz', 'Did you bring the dooinz with ye?'

- My mum called the kerb the 'cribbin', and if someone looked grumpy or raging you would say, 'He had a bake on him like a slapped arse' ('bake' = face).

- Mum would get me all happed up in a warm coat, hat and scarf and call me 'Johnny-Forty-Coats'.

- When I asked what was for dinner, she always, always answered, 'Shame a hate.' I still haven't met anyone else who knows that phrase.

- 'Look at the time and not a child in the house washed!' was another one.

I still use all these and more and now so do my wains (kids).

December

So, to our twelfth month, derived from Latin 'decem', meaning ten. As with September, October and November, our last
four months are misnomers and yet misnomers, inaccuracies,
errors, misappellations that no one is bothered by.

It has to be said, there is something amusing about the
fact that Latin is often used in, say, science, law and medicine with the effect in modern usage of sounding accurate,
precise and official. Think of people reeling off the Latin
names of plants, parts of the body or official legal concepts
like 'sub judice'. And yet every day, hiding in the names of
our months, we are two months out with our nomenclature.

Interestingly, the word 'December' doesn't put in an
appearance in the modern English names for the Western
December festivals: Christmas Eve, Christmas Day, Boxing
Day and New Year's Eve.

The Venerable Bede tells us that in Old English this
time was called Ġēolamonaþ or 'Yule-month'. Across the
Germanic peoples, ancient and modern, there are many
accounts of Yule festivals, sacrifices, booze-ups and much
enjoyment. Winter in the Northern Hemisphere was a tough
time for thousands of years for people relying on animal
skins, wood fires and preserved foods to see them through till
spring. The supermarket Yule log is a chocolatey remnant of
these wild occasions.

The word 'December' though, can be used as a metaphor
for various kinds of coldness, as Shakespeare knew when
he wrote Sonnet 97. Even at the height of 'summer's time',
the speaker in the poem is feeling 'remov'd' from his loved
one through 'absence', so it feels like 'old December' with

its 'freezings', 'dark days' and 'bareness'. '[T]he very birds are mute / Or if they sing, 'tis with so dull a cheer ...' Even thinking of 'teeming autumn' is no comfort as it seems to be nothing more than 'the hope of orphans'.

So December can be a mark or sign of absence and cold.

How like a winter hath my absence been
From thee, the pleasure of the fleeting year!
What freezings have I felt, what dark days seen!
What old December's bareness everywhere!
And yet this time remov'd was summer's time,
The teeming autumn, big with rich increase,
Bearing the wanton burthen of the prime,
Like widow'd wombs after their lords' decease:
Yet this abundant issue seem'd to me
But hope of orphans and unfather'd fruit;
For summer and his pleasures wait on thee,
And thou away, the very birds are mute;
Or if they sing, 'tis with so dull a cheer
That leaves look pale, dreading the winter's near.

Here's another Rosen favourite. My brother and I were once poking things down a drain in the street and a woman came by and shouted at us (heavy warning voice): 'You'll get scarlet fever!'

My brother and I made it a catchphrase for any time either of us were doing anything tricky: 'You'll get scarlet fever!'

'I used to sit on the cold doorstep. A warning from my Nan: "You'll get king cough in your bum." I had no idea what it meant but now think it referred to haemorrhoids!'

@GranBERoY

'If I made a mistake sewing, my mother would say: "A blind man on a galloping horse wouldn't see that."'

@JeanChapple1

'When sitting down with a cup of tea after working in the garden, my grampy used to say, "That's better, Maureen" (my nan), which I still say, to the bemusement of my children.'

@samshep

'My mother often used to feel put upon, and her empathetic neighbour's response was always "The willing horse gets flogged", a phrase my siblings and I like to repeat – sounds best with a sigh.'

@bolandini

'When you were somewhere dark and the light was turned off my dad would say, "It's dark inside this tiger." I think it is a *Goon Show* quote. I always say this now.'

@Rutherfordcare

'On a visit to my aunt in America, who was describing making sausage skins from the entrails from her recently slaughtered cow, she said, "They were still warm, and that's the best bit."

A phrase we still repeat to describe something quite horrible.'

@DRobertsonRN

Another memory of my father, Harold Rosen, who would always say, 'Can't eat stewed fruit, lad, gives me the squitters.' My brother and I loved walking round the house, imitating our father saying that.

'My uncle Albert, a Norfolk man, used to excuse himself when going to the toilet for a wee by saying he was "going to strain his tates".'

Linda Whitney

'Going to the loo was always going to see a man about a dog.'

David Cohen

'A work colleague tells us he's off to "turn my bike around".'

@RPBlackburn

My son says he's just going off to 'squeeze the cheese'. A friend says he's going to 'strain the greens'.

'If the house was messy, my gran always used to say, "It's like Stainshall Bank Fair!" I only found out last year that it was a corruption of Stagshaw Bank Fair – a real event renowned for drink and debauchery. So, not really like our front room.'

@AndromedaDurham

'One I doubt was used outside our family. Any time my room was untidy (always), it was described as looking like "Shuff Bentley's yard". I think said yard was one of those post-war scrapyards that had everything, in bits.'

@Envizage

When the Rosen family's dishwasher broke down, my mother started calling it the 'wishdasher'.

'When annoyed, my dad used to exclaim "Bloody Walsall." Or, occasionally, "Bloody Nora." No idea why.'

@Karen_committed

My great-grandfather (Jewish, living in Amsterdam) used to say, "Don't think with your head on my shoulders" as a response to unsolicited advice.'

Tara Fraser

'Never stir the pot, you'll have ginger twins!'

@Londonlintin

'My husband's grandmother, when required to help one of the grandchildren take their jumper off, would give the instruction: "Hands up for Jesus!" It's stuck in the family and it's all I can do to hold my tongue at school when one of the children asks for help.'

@katherinecavey

My own father once explained to me that there was a very good reason to change the usual expression to 'If a job's worth doing, it's worth doing badly' – but I've forgotten his explanation.

'It's cold enough for a fur-lined walking stick!'

@KathrynScorah

What's wrong with saying that?

As you'll know by now, I'm learning a language – it's the language my grandparents spoke and probably all the people going back for many generations before them: Yiddish. People ask me why am I learning it? I think we can have many reasons for learning a language: it's interesting to see and hear the roots of what it is we say. In my case, my parents said a lot of things because of the things their parents said. To study that language is a way of getting into their heads. It was actually my mother's first language, something I only found out when we went to Germany in 1957. We were sitting at a table being served drinks and my mother looked up and said, 'I understand everything they're saying.'

I asked her how, and that was when she said that for the first five years of her life, she only spoke Yiddish. There's enough similarity between Yiddish and German to make them 'mutually intelligible' for quite a lot of the time. I had thought that it was our father who knew Yiddish and German because he was the one who scattered Yiddish and German expressions through his speech. Why had Mum been so reserved about it?

I'm also interested in language and languages anyway. I very much like finding out about word families – even with that very basic word 'the'. In Yiddish and German there are several ways of saying what grammarians call 'the definite article', depending on what word they come in front of and where in an expression it comes. If I was writing one of these in English, it would sound like this: 'dee'. If you say 'the' and 'dee' you can feel your tongue doing something very similar for the 'd' and 'th' sound. In fact, many speakers of English all over the world do make a 'd' sound when saying 'the' anyway. This tiny, seemingly trivial example is one of thousands and thousands of word families across many languages. Some linguists use these word families to construct the languages that people spoke thousands of years ago and to chart the movement of peoples around the world. It's a bit like the DNA of languages.

Another reason for my learning Yiddish (though this could be the same for any language) is to experiment with my memory. At the time of my writing this I'm 78. Can a 78-year-old brain learn? I can answer that: yes, it can – slowly.

What I'm saying is that my reasons for learning Yiddish are a mix of personal, cultural, intellectual and scientific – if that doesn't sound too pompous. As we learn a song, or a point of grammar, there are moments when I feel a flood of emotion. I feel that I am with my mother or father. I say a phrase like 'gut yontev' – it means 'have a good holiday' (say 'gut' as if you come from Yorkshire and the 'ev' ending is more like an 'uh' followed by 'f') – and it feels as if I'm with my father, or even being my father. If we talk about food, as the words come up, I can hear a conversation from a moment 70 years ago when we're all at home, sitting round the kitchen table (cholent is a lamb and barley dish; bubbe means granny):

My father says, 'Ah, cholent.
I loved cholent.'
And Mum says, 'Why do you go on about cholent?'
And he says,
'Ah, my bubbe's cholent.'

We look from one to the other.
What's going on here?

Then Mum says,
'If you think I'm going to stand by the cooker
For hours and hours on end cooking cholent
Like your bubbe did,
You've got another think coming to you.
Your bubbe spoiled you.
You were spoiled.
Remember,
I'm
Not
Your
Bubbe.'

And our father would turn to us and say,
'What did I say?
What did I say wrong?
All I said was that I liked my bubbe's cholent.
What's wrong with saying that?'

So just saying the word 'cholent' in a Yiddish class in 2024, brings back a conversation from 70 years before, a conversation in which my parents are talking about someone (my father's grandmother) who was born in Poland in 1862.

By the way, I'm not sure that my father ever did find out what was 'wrong' about him going on about his bubbe's cholent.

Christmas

One feature of Christmas in times past were mummers' plays. These are rhyming plays usually acted by local people and often telling the story of St George and the Dragon. When St George is killed, a doctor is summoned. Here's one example of how the doctor speaks to Father Christmas and the assembled audience (as collected by G.A. Rowell, probably in Kirtlington in the nineteenth century):

Father Christmas:
> And what can'st thou cure?

Doctor Brown:
> The hitch, the stitch, the stone, the palsy and the gout,
> The pains within and the pains without,
> The molygrubs, the polygrubs,
> and those little rantantorius diseases.
> Let the wrinkles break
> Or the palsy quacke.
> Take one of my pills and try them.
> Bring any old woman unto me that has been dead
>   seven years,
> in her coffin eight,
> and buried nine.
> If she's only got one hollow rum turn serum turn old
>   jack tooth
> in the back of her head.
> If she can only manage to crack one of my little pills
> I'll be bound in the bond of a thousand pounds
> to maintain her back to life again.
> This is the case that was never before,
> But now, King George, rise up and fight once more.

Those of us who love the nonsense poetry of Edward Lear and Lewis Carroll must bear in mind that people created nonsense speech and nonsense verses before either of them appeared on the scene – which Shakespeare tried to capture with the character of Lear's Fool in *King Lear*.

2 5

The site Buzzfeed has logged some interesting Christmas requests from children:

'My seven-year-old wants Santa to turn her into a dog for 24 hours so she can "do dog things" and understand our family pet.'

'At school, my six-year-old brother had to write a letter to Santa. He asked for a weekend!'

Wendy Cope famously wrote:

Bloody Christmas, here again.
Let us raise a loving cup;
Peace on earth, goodwill to men,
And make them do the washing up.

2 6

Boxing Day

Why Boxing Day?

The *OED* gives the first entry for Boxing Day as 1743, the day after Christmas when 'better-off' people traditionally gave boxes (gifts) to people who had helped them, such as tradespeople or servants.

Before this, there had been a long tradition of there being an alms box in churches and it was customary for people to put money in that box – possibly on the Feast of St Stephen, which is 26 December.

Parents who give their children boxing gloves can interpret the phrase differently, and they should give tissues to mop up the blood from bleeding noses.

Boxing Day is the traditional day for board games, a misspelling of bored games (just in case you believe me: not really). When some people play board games that rely on the rolling of dice or what letters you take out of the sack when playing Scrabble, they become superstitious and imagine that the roll of the dice or the letters in the sack are geared against them. My father was like that. I only have to play Scrabble now and an image comes up in front of me of my father pulling letters out of the bag, squealing and sighing in agony: 'Would you believe it?!' 'Every one a vowel!' 'I'm not going to be able to make a single word!' 'Disaster!'

My mother would tell him to shuttup and he always won anyway.

As we come close to the end of the book, here are some fare-well sayings …

'"If I don't see thee through't week, I see thee through't window." Used when saying goodbye to a friend. An old bloke at the pub used to say it, and my parents always said this too … we still say it to family members when we say goodbye.'

@johnstephen76

'My Lancashire grandma's usual form of goodbye was, "Si thi on t'flypaper" (see you on the flypaper).'

@sue_lees

'We went "up the wooden hill to blanket street" at bedtime.'
@astitchinglife

And a farewell from the Rosen household. My mother said every night, 'Goodnight, muzhik', which means 'man' or 'peasant' in Polish. Also, as endearment: 'shmerel', which is a little fool.

She would also call out, 'Where's my hat, I'm going?' as she left the house, the point being she didn't have a hat.

How many of the words of 'Auld Lang Syne' do you know?

Do you know what it means?

And first of all, who's it by?

It was written down by Robert Burns in 1788, but as with a lot of the great Burns's work, he adapted songs and poems that he heard and collected.

'Auld lang syne' literally means 'old long since' or, as we might say, 'a long time ago' or even 'once upon a time'.

Here's Burns's version, with glossary in square brackets.

How's that for convenience?

Should auld acquaintance be forgot,
And never brought to mind?
Should auld acquaintance be forgot,
And auld lang syne?

Chorus:
For auld lang syne, my jo, [my dear]
For auld lang syne,
We'll tak' a cup o' kindness yet,
For auld lang syne.

And surely ye'll be your pint-stoup! [you'll buy your
    pint-cup]
And surely I'll be mine!
And we'll tak' a cup o' kindness yet,
For auld lang syne.

Chorus

We twa hae run about the braes [we two have run about
    the hills]
And pou'd the gowans fine; [and plucked the daisies fine]
But we've wander'd mony a weary fit [many a weary foot]
Sin' auld lang syne. [since auld lang syne]

Chorus

We twa hae paidl'd in the burn [we two have paddled in
    the stream]
Frae morning sun till dine;
But seas between us braid hae roar'd [broad have roared]
Sin' auld lang syne.

Chorus

And there's a hand, my trusty fiere! [friend]
And gie's a hand o' thine! ['gie's' = give us]
And we'll tak' a right gude-willie waught [goodwill draught]
For auld lang syne.

Chorus

A FINAL NOTE

In the beginning was the word
And the word is ours:
The names of places,
The names of flowers,
The name of names,
Words are ours.
Page-turners
For early learners
How to boil an egg
Or mend a leg
Words are ours
Wall charts
Love hearts
Sports reports
Short retorts
Jam-jar labels
Timetables
Following the instructions
For furniture constructions
Ancient mythologies
Online anthologies
Who she wrote for
Who to vote for
Joke collections
Results of elections
Words are ours
The tale's got you gripped

Have you learned your script?
The method of an experiment
Ingredients for merriment

W8n 4 ur txt
Re: whts nxt
Print media
Wikipedia
Words are ours
Subtitles on TV
Details on your CV
Book of great speeches
Guide to the best beaches
Looking for chapters
On velociraptors
Words are ours
The mystery of history
The history of mystery
The views of news
The news of views
Words to explain
The words for pain
Doing geography
Autobiography
Arabian Nights
Fighting for your rights
What to do in payphones
Goodbyes on gravestones
Words are ours.

Map your language

Many books about language describe language 'out there'. Of course, it is 'out there' but, give it a moment's reflection, it's also 'in here' – in us, in our minds, and in our everyday meetings with all the people of our life. I hope that in this book I've showed the joy and fun of looking at language 'in here', the phrases and words we love, that stick in our minds because they're from us.

When I say it's in our mind, this means many different things. It seems as if we can think without language but many of our thoughts are in and with language. These can be memories of what people say, or things we've read or things we've heard. We can also imagine in language: plans, hopes, visions of how things might turn out. They can be reflections on what is going on right now, as we perceive them through our eyes, ears, nose, touch and taste.

But let's turn back to 'memories of what people say'. This is a rich and powerful matter that plays a huge part of how we think about who we are as people. In fact, the moment we start to think of our parents, grandparents, siblings, school friends, teachers, the books we've read, the movies and TV programmes we've enjoyed, it becomes an enormous resource or archive of language. And it's an archive that can feel as if it's 'me' or 'us'. It's both a community of influences in our heads and something individual, at one and the same time.

This has always felt central to my understanding of what language is and who it's for. I also think it's a great place to start thinking about language. If we start here, it can hold back our temptation to talk about language as if it's some kind of crea-ture or machine that can do stuff all on its own. I know I've heard myself saying things like: 'English changed rapidly in the fourteenth century'. Did it? What does that actually mean? Surely it wasn't 'English' that changed because 'English' isn't a thing on its own, separate from people. What happened was that people changed how they spoke and wrote. What we call language (or any given language) is always language-in-use, or English-in-use and so on.

As proof of this, where better to start than with language 'in here'.

So how best to grasp this? We can consult our 'resource' – our archive – and one way to do this is to create our own 'language maps'.

This is a flexible, growing history of how you speak and write – with the implication that it's an explanation for why you speak and write in the way you do. Because it explains this about you as an individual, I think it will go on to explain (or at the very least, illustrate) how and why we all speak and write in the ways we do. We are in a sense a species walking about with intertwined language maps.

In the jargon, by doing this, you are exploring your 'idiolect' (the language you personally have and use) and you're doing this by reaching into the 'sociolects' you know. That's to say, reaching into the kinds of language produced by the language groups that you've lived with and known.

By the way, there are other kinds of language map that tell fascinating stories too – like a map of all the place names in the British Isles that have Scandinavian parts in the names. If you see a map of these, they give us an idea of where the people we usually call the 'Vikings' settled. I've seen a map for the areas where children said (or used to say) the different kinds of 'truce words' like 'fainites', 'fainies' or 'croggies' when playing catch ('he', 'it', 'tig'). There are other maps showing where people use the words for the different names for alleyways ('alley', 'ginnel', etc.) or different ways in which people pronounce (or don't pronounce) the 'r' sound.

This map, though, is of you. If you've enjoyed this book, maybe you'd like to have a go at mapping your own language.

One way to start is to make a spidergram.

You put yourself in the middle – as a circle, or your name, or a photo, or self-portrait –however you want.

Then you draw lines out from you. These lines are like vectors, lines along which words have come to you. You've responded to those words by remembering them and using them. You can remind yourself of this two-way traffic by putting arrow marks on each line, facing in both directions.

Now, what's on the end of these lines? The significant places and people where you've encountered language that is important to you.

You start off by being very spare. Draw each of these places and people as boxes.

Into the boxes you put a significant word or phrase that is connected to that place or person that tells you something to do with the language from that time. It's a word or phrase that you've inherited and that you think explains something significant or interesting to do with how you speak, write and think.

As an example, here's mine. (You've met some of these earlier in the book.) I'm not offering you this because it's particularly interesting. Quite the opposite: these language maps are usually only interesting for you and people you know well, like people in your family. Think of them as a language photo album.

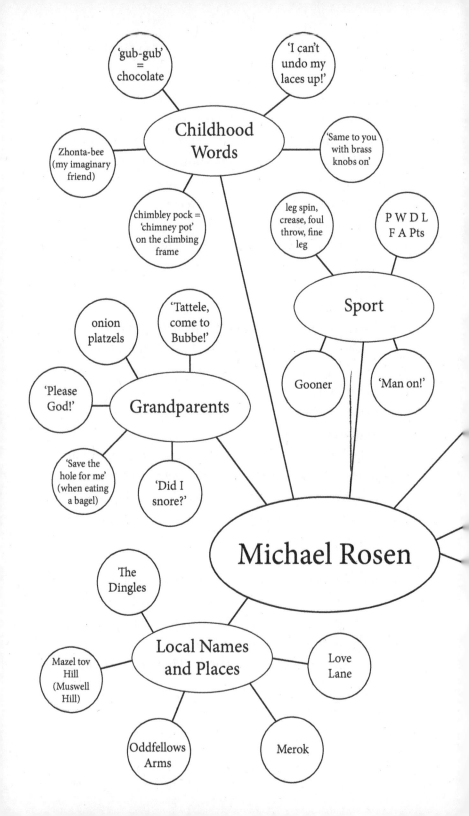

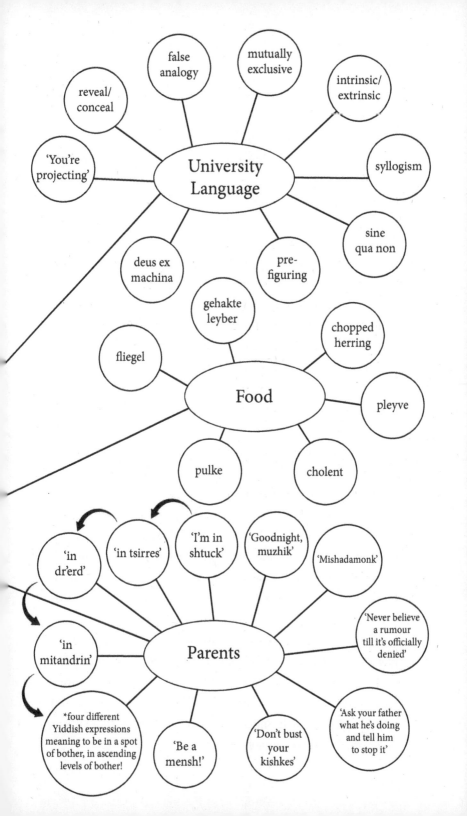

University Language

- reveal/conceal
- 'You're projecting'
- false analogy
- mutually exclusive
- intrinsic/extrinsic
- syllogism
- sine qua non
- pre-figuring
- deus ex machina

Food

- gehakte leyber
- fliegel
- chopped herring
- pleyve
- pulke
- cholent

Parents

- 'in dr'erd'
- 'in tsirres'
- 'I'm in shtuck'
- 'Goodnight, muzhik'
- 'Mishadamonk'
- 'Never believe a rumour till it's officially denied'
- 'in mitandrin'
- *four different Yiddish expressions meaning to be in a spot of bother, in ascending levels of bother!
- 'Be a mensh!'
- 'Don't bust your kishkes'
- 'Ask your father what he's doing and tell him to stop it'

As I said, probably not very interesting for you, but very interesting to me.

I'm suggesting that you do something similar, now.

I'm also suggesting that as you do this, you will start to find out some important things about language. Please do your language map before you read on.

Language belongs to people

As I said at the outset, my map reminds me that language belongs to people. We might say, 'A lot of Americanisms have come into English.' In a way, that's nonsense. Americanisms didn't fly in and walk about. People chose to say or write certain kinds of words and expressions that they had heard or read. In fact, you can chart some of these changes in your own language map. The chances are that the way your parents or grandparents speak/spoke is different from the way you speak.

This may sound pedantic but it's because we have this idea that English is a 'thing' so firmly in our heads, that we end up thinking that English or parts of English can do things on their own. We say things like, 'In the phrase "blue sky", the word "blue" modifies the word "sky".' Again, it may seem pedantic, but in fact, the word 'blue' can't 'do' anything. It's the use of the word 'blue' in that particular way, by millions of people, over hundreds of years, that enables me on this occasion to make it affect or modify the word 'sky'.

Then again, the word 'English' (meaning the language) is just a term to describe how millions of people choose to speak and write. People who write about language sometimes express views on English. They might say, 'You shouldn't speak and write English in such-and-such a way,' as if 'English' exists as an entity outside of ourselves.

So the problem with thinking that language is a thing is that we easily lapse into thinking that languages are something like taxis, moving about the surface of the earth, taking on passengers and dropping others off. Here's an example: I might say, 'He went on and on about it ad nauseam.' The 'taxi' way of talking about that is to say, '"Ad nauseam" is Latin; it's the Latin passenger that the taxi English has taken on board.' In fact, English didn't take on board anything because it can't. What's happened is that first some people, then more people, then even more people liked saying 'ad nauseam'. This leads us straight to the really interesting stuff: who started saying it? And, why did more and more people start saying it? And then, why are people still saying it?

Making creoles

The other problem with the 'taxi' view of a language is that it's separate from other taxis, cars and trucks. In fact, the history of the way we speak and write is full of examples of people in large numbers speaking what we describe as 'different languages' at the same time as one language. One term for two or more languages in one is 'creole'.

In fact, there's a way of talking about English as having been a creole. Just in case you don't know the story, here goes: it would seem that in 1065, the majority language being spoken and written (with many variations and dialects) in the British Isles is what we call Old English. The reason why there were many variations and dialects being spoken and written is because the people speaking had their origins from various places around the north-west of Europe and Scandinavia. These were people we now call (in modern English) Saxons, Angles, Jutes, Franks, Frisians and Scandinavians including people from Iceland. There were several Celtic languages being spoken too which I'll leave to one side. One effect of people converting to Christianity was that they also used Latin words taken from Latin versions of the Bible. That was 1065.

Then, a year later, an army from Normandy won the Battle of Hastings. The Normans spoke Norman French and used that language when they took power. Just in case we jump to the conclusion that Norman French was some kind of 'pure' French, we have to bear in mind that Norman is a way of saying 'Norse men'. So the people in what we now call France adapted the Latin spoken by the Romans, incorporating the Celtic languages spoken before the Romans arrived. The Norman French people combined some of the Norse ways of speaking to make Norman French.

Now, leap forward to just over 300 years later, and Geoffrey Chaucer wrote *The Canterbury Tales*.

It's a creole. As you go through each line of *The Canterbury Tales* you can identify which words and grammar owe their origins to the language spoken in 1065 and which to the Normans in 1066. The 'taxi' way of talking about this is to say, 'which words are English and which words are French'. What I'm suggesting though is that this overlooks (ignores, even) how at any given moment, people speak in multi-lingual, multi-dialectal ways. Some people describe that as 'English and French merged', but my point is that it's not languages doing the merging, it's people doing it. Us.

If you glance back at my language map, you'll see examples of that. I hear the phrase 'in shtuck' being used by people who have no familial relationship with Jewish people. 'In shtuck' is a phrase that some people who speak English have grown to like, along with, say, 'keeping shtum', 'lovely nosh', 'shlock of the new' and many others. If you've got non-

English relatives on your map, maybe you can see the process of people mixing languages and dialects in action too.

This leads to some interesting questions: how did our parents and grandparents use those words and expressions that we might label as 'regional' or 'local' or 'non-English' or 'non-British'? Was this just between ourselves? Did we use them when we knew that other people outside of our family group would understand them? In other words, did we use them with people we identified as part of our cultural, ethnic, religious group? And, importantly, did we not use them when we were with people who wouldn't or didn't understand them?

We can write this information on our language maps.

Variation in one person's language

The answers to those questions tell us that in addition to the fact that the language we speak is not a thing, it is also not just 'one thing'. That's to say, we all speak and write in ways that are different from the ways in which other people speak and write. And we do this for different purposes. In the jargon, we operate using different 'registers' and 'codes'. We might also say that you or a person you might know is 'bi-dialectal', though many of us (all of us, probably) hop between two or more dialects, sometimes called 'code-switching'. Again, go back to my language map, and you can see what we might term, variously, as slang, jargon, scientific language, formal language as well as that use of Yiddish. This reminds us that, though I might say when I'm in France, or when I'm filling in a form, 'I speak English', this conceals something much more varied than that term implies. The term 'English' doesn't really cover these diverse uses. I speak and write 'Englishes'.

And there's yet another problem with thinking of 'English' or 'language' as a thing: there is a hidden assumption that any language (but let's stick with English for the moment) has some kind of core way of being spoken and this is the 'proper way' and that everything else is a deviation from it. You'll hear people say, for example, 'she speaks with a dialect' or 'she has a very strong accent'. The truth is that we all speak with a dialect, we all speak with an accent. It's just that the word 'dialect' is often used in a disguised way to mean 'regional' or 'local'. If you think now of anyone you know who you think of as not having an accent, almost certainly that person is someone who speaks with what the jargon calls the 'standard' form in your part of the English-speaking world. There are in fact, 'standard' ways of speaking English in England, Wales, Scotland, Ireland, the USA, Australia and so on and these are all different. Then within those countries, there are many dialects and accents as well as the 'standard' ones. That's to say, millions and millions of people all over the world speaking English in different ways.

Just to be clear, these different dialects and accents don't all have the same status in society. What's more, the status of these accents and dialects doesn't stay the same over time. As I write this, I'm 78 years old. In my lifetime, I know that I hear accents used by presenters of, say, news and current affairs programmes that you wouldn't and couldn't have heard in England 60 years ago. Imperceptibly, some accents were promoted from not-acceptable to acceptable. Interestingly, some non-standard accents were in my childhood more 'permissible' than others. So there were Irish, Welsh and Scots news presenters but not anyone with a marked Birmingham, Cockney or Geordie accent.

This probably tells us some things about language, accent, dialect and class – or perceived class. Your own language map may reveal some of this. It might be interesting to put on your map what people in your family or school said to you about language.

Did people try to correct you, and tell you to speak in a way that was different from how you and your friends spoke? Was that connected to class or perceived class? And were they successful? Did they succeed in getting you to change the way you spoke?

On that matter, it was a great mystery to me how it was that my parents spoke very differently from their own parents, siblings and some of the friends they had grown up with. If I paint that with broad brush strokes, I'd say that their parents, siblings and some of their friends spoke with clearly marked London accents, but by the time they were bringing me up, my parents spoke most of the time much more closely to 'standard' or what we used to call 'BBC English'. How did they do it? If I do a bit of family archaeology, I might reconstruct their childhood accents as having been London Cockney with Yiddish 'inflection' or 'intonation' – that was the music of their speech, along with many Yiddish words and expressions. In other words, not only do we speak English in several ways in our everyday lives, but we also change the way we speak over time. One of the most interesting programmes I ever presented as part of *Word of Mouth* was with an expert in phonetics (the science of how we speak). He played recordings of Queen Elizabeth II from her very first Christmas broadcast to her most recent. He then isolated some vowel and consonant sounds and showed how the Queen had changed these over time. If we wanted to identify these changes, the Queen had moved some of her accent from that of a very small social group nearer to one that was much bigger. Some might say, she moved 'down' the social ladder in some of the very specific ways in which she pronounced some of her vowels and consonants.

Again, you might be able to reveal some of these kinds of language journeys on your map.

Theme

On my language map, I identified such things as food and sport. These are examples which remind us that we produce language in theme-specific ways. That's to say, when we speak and write, we are writing on a theme or topic. That might seem obvious but there is a way in education, for example, of treating language as being not theme-specific. That's to say, it's just language. We put sentences and incomplete sentences in front of students and ask the students to describe them, name them, name the parts of them, complete them, etc. without any reference to the theme. This may not matter in the context of an exercise or test, but perhaps such lessons imply that language can float free of what it is people are trying to say and why. In real life, away from these exercises and tests, people are talking to each other on a topic or in relation to a topic in some way or another. If you look at your language map, you should be able to see that the examples you gave come from a situation in which you or others were talking about or around a topic or theme. You could perhaps add these.

Genre

As part of this, there's an interesting matter of genre. There's an argument for saying that the moment we speak or write we are in effect producing language according to a kind of pre-ordained shape. We use the word 'genre' often to describe, say, a type of film, like a rom-com. We might say, for example, that this latest film starring, let's say, George Clooney is a

rom-com with a twist, or that the usual 'elements' or 'ingredients' of a rom-com were there, apart from, for instance, the
obstacle to the couple getting together, or some such. In other
words, we are saying that there is some kind template or blue-
print hiding behind the movie we're watching that this film is
mostly conforming to.

Well, there's a way of thinking of language like this. You
walk into a shop. You ask if they have something. The shop
assistant answers you. This may all seem very operational
and matter-of-fact but in a way you're doing something
that's already been scripted. At least, the outlines have been
scripted. If you walk into a clothes shop where you've never
been before, go over to the shop assistant who you've never
met before and the first thing you ask them about is whether
they think opening a chess game by moving pawn to K4 is a
good idea, you've broken out of both the topic and a genre
and into another one. Looking back at a moment from my
childhood, I often think of our teacher standing in the middle
of the classroom at the time of the 11-plus exam, which would
decide whether we would go to grammar school or not, saying,
'All of you on this side of the class will fail, and all of you on
that side of the class will pass.' One reason I remember this so
vividly is not only because of how this seemed so determinis-
tic and discriminatory. It's also because it was genre-busting.
Miss Williams was very interested in instruction. Fair enough.
She was also very interested in discipline. Fair enough. That's
all in-genre. But I think that day she stepped out of genre in
order to give us a running commentary on how the whole
system was working (or supposedly working). There was no
instruction or discipline going on.

Conversations

Hiding in my map, and perhaps in yours, is that all the examples are embedded in conversations: conversations with my grandparents, parents, brother, friends, teachers, fellow sports-lovers and so on. Now here's something very strange: you can open hundreds of books about language, and you will hardly ever find descriptions or analyses of conversations. It's as if words, phrases and expressions along with the matter of how languages change exist in some kind of word-corridor. Words are described as changing from, say, 'bringeth' to 'bring'. The places where those words changed were mostly in people's conversations. The reason why in a Shakespeare play we hear such a phrase as 'so doth the company thou keepest' but I never say this in my everyday speech is because millions of people changed the way they spoke in conversations. It's too late now, but if we had a time machine, we could find out why they stopped using 'doth' by interviewing hundreds of people over several hundred years and asking them!

If you go back over your language map, you could perhaps enlarge it by embedding the words and phrases in conversations. Who's speaking to whom? And why? Who's speaking 'at' someone else? Who's speaking 'with' someone else? This little exercise takes the study of language away from the textbook into the conversations of everyday life. We can investigate language by looking at the cogs of social life, where we and our forebears used language to express love, hope, fear, laughter, anger, hunger, pleasure, ambition, depression, youth, age, play and the needs and requirements of work, money and poverty – with other people in conversation.

So if conversation is the crucible in which we make language, how do we make conversations work? Looking at my map, there are already indications – shadows, perhaps –

of very different conversations: my childhood vocabulary – full of jokes, rude rhymes, backslang and the like – comes from a very different context to the language I was taught in university. Being read to in class is a social routine with established rules that are very different from the rules and routines that come with taking part in a play.

Identity

Finally, there's the big question of identity. It's an obvious thing to say but language and identity are very closely intertwined. If you look at your map, you'll see many aspects of people (and you) expressing their identity through language, just as I have in mine. To look more closely at this, I'll take a moment to make clear what I mean by 'language'.

One way to classify the elements of language is to talk of its sound (phonology, which includes questions of pronunciation, accent, intonation), its vocabulary (lexis or words) and its grammar and syntax (how we stick words together to make meaning). Just to complicate things: as we speak, these three elements are all working at the same time. A word is only a word in speech because we hear its sound. A word only has meaning because it's linked to other words through grammar. Tip that on its head, and there is only grammar if there are words that are linked by grammar; in speech the grammar is expressed through the sound of what's being spoken. A word of warning here, though: there are some who maintain that 'grammar' is an abstract rulebook or pattern-book that lies 'behind' everything we say, almost as though it exists without the words using it. Does it?

Back with identity: despite their co-dependence, let's isolate those three elements of language. The sound of how we speak will tell us that we speak with an accent, that we use 'dialect forms' (both in our choice of words and our ways of using grammar), and we create distinctive rhythms and music in how we speak. We may not always be conscious of it, but how we speak is very important to us and our sense of who we are and how we want to be seen in the different situations we live and work.

What's more, clearly, the way others see us is greatly affected by how we speak. They will describe us as being, say, 'West Country' or 'Scots', even if we do or don't describe ourselves like that, or we might qualify what others say in ways that feel important to us, saying something like, 'Well, actually I'm from the Highlands,' or some such. Or people may get it wrong: 'Are you Jamaican?' 'No, I'm British but I was born in Trinidad.'

At various times in our lives, it may well become more or less important that we identify with the sound of what we think of as our origins. If we move and migrate, this may well affect us in many ways too. Some people can flip between the sound of their speech in the place they have moved to and the sound of their speech when they go 'home' to where they were brought up. In other words, people are able to flip according to who they are with.

Again, obviously, the words we use are inseparably inter-twined with who we think we are and how we think of ourselves. Your language map should, I hope, tell you in very specific ways how that works.

Here, it might be useful to think of how we carry words in our heads. It's bit more complicated than first appears. There are the words we use a lot every day – let's say the word 'hand'. There are words we use in special circumstances and so not very often – perhaps you're very interested in running, so you might refer to your 'patella'. There are words we understand but we hardly ever use ourselves: this happens as we listen to the radio or watch TV. We hear something from a culture different from ours, an activity we don't take part in, someone from a different generation; we learn what it means but it doesn't become part of the way we speak. Before *Strictly Come Dancing* became a mass entertainment, there weren't many people who knew the names of the different dance moves, let alone the different dances. Millions know them now but it won't be millions using them in their everyday speech.

This should be made a bit more complicated by talking of 'expressions' and 'phrases'. Look at your language map. Have you included expressions and phrases as well as words? We should. That's because, in a way, it's wrong to think of ourselves as talking in words! If you look at that sentence: 'That's because, in a way, it's wrong to think of ourselves as talking in words', you can see that there are segments or chunks there, like: 'that's because', 'in a way', 'to think of ourselves', 'as talking' and 'in words'. Maybe you would chop it up in different chunks? Even so, you can see that each of 'in' and 'a' and 'way' have very little meaning, but 'in a way' is a meaningful chunk. Same with the other phrases.

This means that though we often talk about language as being made up of words, in actual fact, when we are using language, we are operating in chunks, phrases, expressions and (in speech) in linked exchanges like: 'You going out?' 'Yep.' You'll know that one kind of book some of us find useful is a 'phrase book'. In other words, it's all very well having a dictionary to tell us what a French word is (for example) but if we can learn a phrase like 'à la carte', it might be more useful for a start than knowing what each of those words ('à', 'la' and 'carte') means.

So it's not just that we mark our identity out with the individual words that we use but it's also very much the matter of what expressions we use. When I was at secondary school, we had a geography teacher who, we thought, had a very distinctive way of speaking. As is often the case, though, we couldn't quite figure out what was distinctive about it. I was given the job of making out that I was sitting in class taking detailed notes on geography from what he was saying, when in actual fact, I was creating a chart to count the particular expressions (and clichés) he was using. One of these was the phrase 'set-up'. I discovered that whether he was describing the population of Switzerland, the erosion of cliffs or pattern of settlement in Lancashire, each one of these was a 'set-up'. 'You've got the Swiss alpine set-up'; 'here's the set-up with wind erosion'; or 'the valleys are important in the Lancashire set-up' and so on. Each time he said 'set-up', I gave it a tick. At the end of the lesson we pored over my chart to see which of his many very ordinary expressions got the highest score. His lessons became utterly fascinating for completely the wrong reason.

Then what about grammar, syntax and identity? For argument's sake, let's say 'grammar and syntax' means several things: it's how we stick words together into expressions and sentences; it's how we converse, linking what you say to what I say; it's how we 'morph' words by adding bits on, taking bits off, changing the sounds of them so that they mean different things as with, say, 'approve', 'disapprove', 'approval'/'disapproval', 'approbation', or with 'walk', 'walks', 'walked' and 'walking'. We can also say that it's how we create meanings across many expressions and sentences, with what is called 'cohesion'. One example of this: 'Michael's writing a book. It's going OK, so far.' The word 'it' only makes sense because it's linked to and expresses or 'stands in for' the word 'book' (cohesion across two sentences). But also there's the expression 'so far' in that second sentence. This also links to 'Michael's writing a book' through a sense of the progression of time. How we indicate the passing of time serves to make passages of writing cohesive. It may point at something that might come later – a kind of forward cohesion, as with a phrase like 'he would live to regret it'. These are two of many ways in which when we construct passages of writing, we create cohesion.

Our identities are wrapped with all this. All over the English-speaking world, we have different ways of saying some of the most basic and common things. That's part of our identity. But distinctive features of our identity might be in our grammar as well as the sound and vocabulary. There is the standard English construction that many people use: 'we were'. Many people in London say 'we was'. Again, people speaking standard English say 'she was'. Many people in Yorkshire say 'she were'. Without going into what's 'right' or 'wrong' about such expressions, I think we can say that this has got something – or even a lot – to do with identity. People choose to speak in those ways. As they say it, it feels to them like it's them saying it. It's who they are. There may even be pressure on them not to talk like that – at least in some circumstances – and yet, they go on doing it. And as I've mentioned before, many people 'code-switch'. In some situations they say 'she was' and in others they say 'she were'. We often do that because that's us showing we share some identity with others. A group of people sharing the same 'idiolects' are sharing a 'sociolect'. Again, though, these '-lects' are not things. They are descriptions of people using language in conversations.

Your language map may well show that too.

Looking back over your language map, what's missing? One key feature that's missing in mine is the language of feelings and emotions. How significant is that?! There is of course a huge resource and archive in my head and in all our heads how people have talked to us with and about feelings and emotions. Love, hate, envy, sorrow, irritation, anger, competitiveness, sense of failure, loss … it goes on and on. On our language maps, we can create a 'box' for each of these and explore who said what to us – when? And why? What do they tell us about what kind of person I am/you are?

And what about 'figurative language'? This is how we use language to express how one thing is 'like' another, or how we can represent one thing by making it another. We've created metaphors, similes and personification to do this. If you say 'pull your socks up' to mean 'do better', that's figurative. We all have a great store of figurative expressions in our heads.

But there are some that are a bit harder to track down (metaphor: 'track down'!). If I say, 'I'm getting behind in my work …' I'm using a word that can also be used for saying 'you're behind me'. Being 'behind' in my work is linked to a spatial idea of something physically placed to my rear! Our whole idea of 'progress', life and death, the passing of time, is linked in the culture I live in, with spatial ideas of the past being at my back, out of sight, round the back, at my rear. I spend a lot of time thinking about the past. In fact, my past is hardly ever gone or 'behind' me. It's either right now, or it's even something I think of going towards! I set myself tasks to inhabit my past (daydreaming, etc.) so that I can write about them. I go forwards into my past ('past' is also a metaphor because it has the physical idea of 'it having passed by me').

So what is your figurative landscape? What are the metaphors you live by, as the linguists George Lakoff and Mark Johnson asked. Some more boxes for your language map, methinks!

ACKNOWLEDGEMENTS

Thanks to Beth O'Dea, producer of BBC Radio 4's *Word of Mouth*.

Thanks also to:

Rob Drummond, who I did the original broadcast with.

Sheela Banerjee, author of *What's in a Name?*

My Yiddish teacher, Tamara Micner.

Simon Elmes, the BBC producer who co-created *Word of Mouth* with writer and broadcaster Frank Delaney.

My school and university literature and language teachers: Miss Saville, Miss Green, Mrs Hill, Mr and Mrs Emmans, Miss Joseph, Mr Honan, Mrs Young, Miss Grant, Barry Brown, Mrs Turnbull, Mr Spearman, Mike Benton, Alan Ward, Ian Donaldson, WW Robson, FW Bateson, Dennis Butts, Tony Watkins, Dudley Jones, Margaret Meek Spencer, Ruth Mertens, Jean Webb.

For teaching me close attention to the speech of working people, Ewan MacColl and Charles Parker.

My parents, Connie and Harold Rosen, who talked and wrote about language all their lives, at home, in schools and at universities.

And my brother, Brian, who taught me how to enjoy the tone of voice and expressions of the people we knew.